Relationship Marketing

View From the Top

and

What It Really Takes to Get There

Network Marketing Guide to Massive Success!

Steve Thompson

D1510846

Copyright © 2013 Steve Thompson

Cover design by Killer Covers, New Zealand

Editing & Formatting by Georgina Chong-You, Florida, USA

FROM A PIRATE PUBLISHING, LLC

ISBN:
978-0-9762880-2-2

DEDICATION & ACKNOWLEDGMENTS

After nearly 20 years in Network Marketing, I owe a great deal to the many great leaders that I have worked with and learned from. Perhaps the best way I can thank them is for them to see the results of their guidance, in my work today.

Originally a bit shy, working in MLM encouraged me to develop my skills in Networking, as well as in Persuasive and Motivational Public Speaking and Training.

I look back and realize that much of what is really good in me came from my mother, Ann Lathe Thompson. She said I could, when others said I could not. My best value systems came from her love and support during the early years of my life.

My special thanks to my good friend and coach, Evan Money, for his encouragement and guidance.

I dedicate this book to the many friends I made while developing my Business Skills in Traditional Business and in Network Marketing. I am especially grateful to the Founders, Corporate Team and many Great Leaders in Ambit Energy. After years of working toward Massive Success, it is in this organization that my Business Dreams Came True.

I am delighted to share this story with you and remain dedicated to your Success!

Get Excited, Stay Focused and Never Quit!

To Success,

Steve Thompson
Austin, Texas

Table of Contents

1

My Business Journey

*M*y name is Steve Thompson. I have been an entrepreneur since I was a small child. I was the neighborhood kid with the Bicycle Repair, Lawn Mowing Service and Coaster Building Business. I was always looking for ways to earn my own way. It set me on a path to always be on the lookout for a good business venture.

I was born in San Antonio, Texas to a railroad engineer and a stay at home mother. Together they raised 4 children. I was the youngest. My father had been elected Local Chairman of a railroad labor union and once I was born we relocated to a small East Texas town named Palestine. Small town life was all I knew growing up.

My parents never talked about being in business. While my father and grandfather both worked for the railroad, my mother's family had a history of business. Her grandfather had been the last entrepreneur in our family history. I was not around that part of the family much because they were in Ohio and we were firmly planted in Texas. In addition, my mother had shocked them all when she left home as a young woman and joined the army to help rehabilitate solders wounded in WWII. She met my father at the end of the war and never really reconnected with her family again. I always wonder if early life stories of her grandfather and his success in business had an impact on me.

My father's union later merged with several other unions and he was fortunate to be elected to national office, which relocated us to Houston, Texas. It was a culture shock when at age 15 I left my life in a small town of about 12,000 for a large city and a high school of over 4,000.

Going to high school in Houston made me much more aware of the larger world. It took away the innocence of knowing everyone around and having small town support and replaced it with a need to be strong, self-reliant and independent. That new perspective changed my life.

Music became a big part of my life. I started playing in local rock bands in junior high and continued through out high school and into early college. I paid my own way through college and had to work and conserve to support myself, so soon I was out of the bands and ended up selling the equipment to help support myself.

I took my first regular job at 15, working in a restaurant. I only lasted a few weeks and did not enjoy it. I found a job at a full service gas station and liked that better. I had a passion for cars and motorcycles and found a way to get paid for doing something I enjoyed. I went from that to working in car dealerships and put myself through college working in an auto parts store.

Finding Your Niche

I graduated with a BBA (Marketing) in less than three years. Not because I was smart but because it was more efficient time management along with significant savings.

Even then, I was rebuilding and working on cars and motorcycles. I found a niche buying wrecked motorcycles, rebuilding them, giving them a paint job and selling then for a significant profit. A job alone was not enough for me.

After graduation, I became an outside parts salesman calling on garages, body shops and dairy farms. From that I moved on to working for a chain of auto supply warehouse's selling to auto parts stores. While I enjoyed working for others, I somehow knew that I needed a business of my own. I soon began studying to become a Real Estate Agent and in the process discovered the world of insurance. Although I was not excited about Insurance, I was very intrigued by the Residual Income, the ability to make the sale once, and get paid over and over again.

Soon I was studying Insurance and applying to what I saw as the best Agency System around -- State Farm Insurance. In 1979, just after turning 24, I moved to Austin, Texas to open a Scratch Agency, basically starting an agency without a book of business. Although I went to college 30 miles south of Austin, I had no friends or relatives there. Nonetheless, it was the quality of life I was looking for and I loved the Texas Hill Country!

From the beginning, I saw insurance as a base business that would allow me to also do other things like serving as a Volunteer Fireman, EMT and on the Travis County EMS Committee. I volunteered with other service organizations and built my education and relationships. At 29 I was *Always be on the lookout for a good business venture.* invited to join the board of a local bank and began another part of my life education. Soon I was serving on Marketing and Loan Committees and learning about many other's business and trends. Although the knowledge I gained was exciting, it wouldn't be powerful until I had applied what I had learned.

Thirty was the age that I started an Entertainment Agency specializing in Artist Development and Management along with Production Management. The music I cherished as a teenager had now led me to make it into a business. I could work with the music I loved and make money. I learned a great deal and dabbled with music management until just a few short years ago when my more profitable MLM Career really took off.

A good friend came to me with a business proposition I found intriguing. He owned an Equestrian Center and offered that if I put up the money and helped with marketing, his people would train the horses. Together we would be able to sell them for a profit while also earning money promoting horse shows. With him, I opened a small business, buying, training and selling horses as well as hosting horse shows. Later that same partner and I opened a small Yacht Brokerage Business in San Diego, CA. We focused on the downturn in the economy and had a good run with our company, "Repo Yacht Sales". As the economy improved we sold that business and began to sail up and down the West Coast of California and Mexico. We saw a niche in Puerto Vallarta and soon found ourselves in the Sailing Charter Business. We took advantage of the changes in International Law and filed a Mexican Corporation.

We learned a lot in that business, especially running a foreign company. We again had a few years of success and then local, less expensive competition began to take our business away. My partner stayed in Mexico, married and is raising 2 children while still an entrepreneur running a Commercial Meat Company, "Carnes del Mundo". I still stay in touch with and visit my friend Kyle, as he is one of the instigators that always encouraged my adventurous activities and entrepreneurship. But all the while I stayed in the Insurance Business, Real Estate Investing and Music Management.

My first Network Marketing Experience was as a very part time Herbalife distributer. I was into health and fitness and was intrigued by Mark Hughes, the founder of Herbalife. The way he spoke about living your dreams and his passion for helping others made me want to learn to do the same. I knew nothing about MLM but began to study.

After a couple of years I gave up Herbalife. It was probably a big mistake but I was going through a divorce and my wife wanted the business. She did not realize the work in Network Marketing so it soon died out. I originally planned to start again but grew tired of the products, deliveries and having to always sell and deliver. There had to be a better way!

For the next 10 years I looked at almost everything that come along. Most of them were more products and usually overpriced. In 1996 I discovered Excel Communications. They sold Long Distance Service. It was a Service, not a Product. I was in! However, they were almost eight years old and my timing was not so good. 1996 was their largest ever and I had very little to do with it. The owner frequently talked about someday selling Electricity and that kept us going. It was 10 times the size of long distance, but it did not happen with Excel. I stayed for years and learned a lot. It took me years to get to a six figure annualized income but still I was hooked.

The opening of Canada was very big for me and I learned a lot about new launches and working with other folks, cultures and climates. However, they sold the company again and I did not feel good about the new owners and left. Sure enough, they were gone in no time.

After that I participated in the first year launch of a Skin Care Company despite my promise of never doing another product-based business. I was intrigued with a start up. I learned a lot there. One important thing I learned was to check the backing of the company very closely. Their investors quit putting in money and they begin to pull back. I was gone and a few months later that company was too.

A close friend brought me into the Travel Industry. Soon I was doing well and when the Top Producers of that company decided to start their own, I went with them. We were friends and I knew they were *Great Network Marketers*.

For the next year I had a blast with them and was a Top 20 Money earner in the country. I thought I would never leave. Then I was invited to come meet the owners of Ambit Energy. I had to look. What I saw changed my life.

I always knew that if anyone got in the Energy Business with Network Marketing and did it right, with the right Management Team, Compensation Plan and Tremendous Investor Strength, it would one of the Largest Success Stories in Business History. They were it, and I had to move. Within a month I had wrapped up my affairs at the travel company and was totally focused on building an Ambit Energy Business.

A better way of doing business was my goal!

With Ambit Energy, my dreams have come true. All of my skills, combined with hard work, a lot of nights on the road and some good timing has set me free financially. I have been in MLM for over 19 years. Some good companies and some that were not so good. But I had the street wisdom to recognize a winner, make a commitment and take massive action to get the job done. I never looked back. I made the decision once and this journey is taking me to new heights!

I wish only the same for you!

2

Embrace Wealth!

*F*irst, you have to give yourself permission to become successful and wealthy. Sounds simple, but most people never do. Unless you were born into a wealthy family, it was probably not only never taught or expected, it was discouraged. Let's think about that for a moment.

What were your childhood lessons about money and wealth? Common lessons are:

1. Rich people are just lucky!

2. All rich people live in different circumstances and usually inherited their wealth.

3. Most rich people are somehow, crooked.

4. Money is the root of all evil. So rich people are just bad.

Now let's examine those all too common misconceptions that hold us back in life:

1. Rich people are just lucky!

Show me a "Lucky" rich person and I will show you someone who either worked real hard for their financial success or their ancestors did. And if it was not them, they had better learn these lessons or as history has taught us, the money will not stay (i.e.: the Lottery Winner or person with inheritance that soon finds themselves without money again). **The only way to accumulate and grow wealth is to become personally more valuable and to give that value to others in exchange for wealth.** In other words, become more valuable and earn more money!

This starts and continues with Personal Development. One can seldom control circumstances or other people, but they should control themselves. Personal Leadership Development is not about learning to lead others; it is about learning to lead yourself. We have to focus, have a plan and work on our plan for personal development every day.

Formal Education is great and the best thing it teaches us is how to learn. We must take those skills and put them to work on one of the greatest journeys we could embark on and that is to become better and more valuable through personal development. There are many experts on this subject and they give of their expertise freely. However, they won't force you to learn like your 5th Grade Math Teacher.

Mentors are the most valuable people to us. Frequently I did not know my mentors but simply learned of them and followed their work. Look for mentors that are not only knowledgeable about what they teach, but have the life experience and success to show for it. If you desire good health, learn from those that have it. For a better family life, watch people that have one. To grow spiritually, read and listen to the works of people that not only teach of it but live it daily to build a better and more valuable life. And, if amassing money is important to you (And if it's not, put this book aside and go watch TV!), **never listen to poor people**.

You can't learn it all in a day, a month or even a year. It takes a lifetime of study and work. However, you will become a bit more valuable with every lesson. As with most things, it is important to prioritize your studies.

Now, let's stop for an important lesson taught by Dr. John C. Maxwell, PH.D. I have had the pleasure to not only study John's work for years, but because of that life of study, I have finally gotten to work with and know one of my greatest mentors personally. John teaches that it is important to work on your strengths, not always your weaknesses. That shocked me when I first heard him say so, but I have grown to understand it well. It is important that you learn your strengths and weaknesses. It is not hard, as most of them you know and anyone close to you in life can quickly help you identify the others.

On a scale of 1 – 10, with 1 being you don't inherently possess that ability and 10 meaning you have a God given mastery of the skill. If you are a 2 or 3 and work really hard, you will move it up a point or two and become a 5 or 6. No one comes to a 5 or 6 for leadership so you have not gained much. If you are however a 6 or 7, with hard work and practice you will become an 8 or 9 and the whole world wants to hear what they have to say. I am not saying don't work at all on your weaknesses; just don't make them your constant focus. Focus first on things that will get you great results.

I like to tell stories and although I am a bit shy, I focused many

> I've heard it said that a good public speaker is not without butterflies, he has just taught them to fly in formation!

hours --okay years --on developing the skill of story telling which leads to public speaking success. What I mean by focus is taking speech classes, spending a year in debate, reading books on storytelling and public speaking, listening to great speakers and most importantly, pushing myself to get in front of people and learn from the experience. (Later we will talk about failure being the only path to success!).

Let's not pull any punches. In Network Marketing one of the most valuable skills is Public Speaking. However, I have known many to prosper without that ability by working to surround themselves with good speakers. Do not let this one slide. The ability to express yourself is very important so make it a priority. Some people I know did not have that skill and made it anyway, made it a priority to move from a 2 to a 5 or 6.

Work on your personal development every day. Don't make it haphazard. Set aside 30 minutes or so each day and your life will begin to improve with each lesson. It may start as a chore but it will become a passion. If you are passionate about something it is never really like work.

2. All rich people live in different circumstances and usually inherited their wealth.

Okay, take a moment and reflect on the wealth of your family. Well then, it is going to have to start with you! The good news is **You Can Become Wealthy**. However, it will not be from luck or inheritance or even your environment. It will be from your hard, but smart work. To often people give up because they were just not born in "Lucky Circumstances". Well, neither were most other wealthy people. They became wealthy on purpose!

I had a good start in life. My father worked for the railroad and later became a Labor Leader because of his focus and hard work. He spent almost 50 years in the same work and mastered the skills required. However, he was still trading time for money and you seldom become wealthy doing that. It does not matter if you earn a few dollars an hour flipping burgers or earn thousands as a surgeon; there just aren't enough hours to become financially free.

It is important to work on your strengths, not always your weaknesses.

Financial freedom is having enough money coming in that you can pay all of your bills, give to charity and enjoy your life's interest, without having to work for the money. It is not about millions. It is about having a business or system that works to produce money so you don't have to. As you grow financially, the numbers will increase, and so will the opportunities.

One of the greatest books on the subject is "How Rich People Think" by Steve Siebold. I urge you to not just read some of these books but to study them. That and other books are written by wealthy people that have spent a lifetime studying wealth. Again, choose your mentors.

Is wealth really important? It is a fact of life that your income frequently determines your family's outcome. It determines where you live, where your children go to school and whom they associate with and learn from on a daily basis. It would be nice if we all had wealthy parents. But if it is not you then shouldn't it be your children? I am not saying give them the world on a silver platter, but don't you want to at least give them a head start in life. The great news is, You Can Do It!

3. Most rich people are somehow crooked.

Perhaps you have watched too many gangster movies. They are quite popular in our world. Funny how so many are drawn to stories of those that rob and steal rather than those who toil daily to make the world a better place? I guess it is just not exciting enough for Hollywood!

Let's set the record straight with some reality. Even the movies end with the bad guy dead or going to jail! Life is that way as well. Frequently it is not jail but rather the loss of unearned gains. People that get it dishonestly do not possess the skills to keep it and wealth finds its true home. Chances are great that the wealthy people you meet, gave more value to society than the middle-income people you cling to. It is more work and takes more study to become wealthy. **Wealth is not for the meek or the lazy. Negative people don't live the laws of attraction; they repel it.**

The very word, *Profit*, is frequently used in a negative light. Although the purpose of business is to create profit for its owners or stockholders, people sometimes speak in very negative terms about profit. I grew up in a labor union home. Some folks speak of the company making profits off the hard work of labor as if that was a bad thing. The owners also made the jobs available by investing in the business yet many begrudge that activity. Somehow, they want the income, the jobs, the benefits to the employees and the public, but they want it given for nothing?

In today's political scene there are many that speak of taking profits from the wealthy that earned it with their risk and innovation and give the wealth to those that did not take the chances, invest their capital or create the jobs and economical improvement. And they still expect the wealthy to repeat the process? What gets rewarded gets done. All other behavior is extinguished.

Equating wealth to dishonesty is a common cop out for people that just aren't willing to do the personal work it takes to amass wealth. The formula is available. **Financial Success is available; it's just not free!**

4. Money is the root of all-evil. So rich people are just bad.

First, let's not misquote one of the greatest works of all time, the Bible. The Bible tells us that the worship of money is bad. What is important to understand is that Good People become better with more money? That is where libraries, food banks, universities, medical breakthroughs and all charity come from. Money! Most of the world's richest people spend a great deal of time on their greatest passion, philanthropy. They give their money away to good causes. Why is that? It is because wealthy people have learned to focus on abundance, not scarcity.

Worship Abundance, Not Scarcity! It calls for a big change in how most of us think. Most of society and frequently our governments are all based on scarcity. What can we do without? What can we cut down on to get by? What do you have to give up so your family can live during hard times? I have good news for you. NOTHING!

Ok, I am not saying to waste money or live beyond your means. We will have a whole chapter on that later. What I mean is that we have been granted a world of abundance. Virtually everything we want or need in life is available to us. We simply have to follow the rules. Offer more value and receive more. Become more valuable and you will attract more money. Once you embrace this way of life, it will be easier.

Again, there are great books about developing yourself into a money attracting person. One of the best has been around a long time. "Think and Grow Rich" by Napoleon Hill. I am a huge follower of Robert Kiyosaki and his "Rich Dad, Poor Dad" along with others. Spend some time with these masters and you will learn to think differently. But you have to set out to do so!

Many people dream of wealth or even wish for it. But they either don't know of or won't follow the rules of attracting wealth. Wanting something for nothing is not even a good dream. Remember, lazy won't get you there. However, hard work alone is not the key either.

We have all heard to work smart, but most never really know what that means. I once heard that digging a ditch is hard work but at the end of the day you merely have a whole in the ground. Do so for a lifetime and you have a grave with both ends kicked out. So how do we work smart?

I am a huge believer in Residual Income. Do the work once and get paid over and over. I was lucky and came across the concept early in life and it changed my life. When I found Multi-Level Marketing (MLM) I found the perfect combination of Extreme

Leverage and Residual Income. That's right. You too have made a life-changing discovery, but it takes more than discovery.

3

First, You Have To Be Willing To Work Hard!

*T*here is an old saying that you can either make money or you can make excuses. Or as my good friend Evan Money author of "Take Action Now!" likes to say:

"Making Millions or Making Excuses".

It is not like the proverbial "digging a ditch", but it is hard work. There are no off times for the mind. It has to always be in your thoughts and there is little separation of business and personal life. It is foremost a relationship business and relationships are fostered constantly. You will frequently need to be prepared to jump from off time to business time with the ringing of the phone or beep of a text message. People that don't understand our business frequently ask why I take phone calls from Top Leaders in my organization at all hours of the day and night.

First, I mean it when I say I will be there for you and second, I earn a fortune helping others. Let's break that down a little.

There are no "Business Hours" in Network Marketing. Sure, I take time off and don't answer the phone or respond to text messages, but not during the critical, high value hours. You see, 8 to 5 is when most people are working a job. As most of our Team members are part time, that is when they are trading time for the dollars they must have to live. So, that is when you must take your down time.

After 5 p.m. you must be ready to spring into action. That is when a Leader in MLM is needed the most. Evenings and weekends are usually when you are needed the most. The good news is that these hours along with all of the really hard work only lasts a few years and then **You Have The Rest of Your Life Off!** Not willing to do that? Stay small in MLM. Put aside your dreams of being a Top Money Earner, keep your job and make only a little extra in your Network Marketing Business. That is what most people do and there is nothing wrong with it. However, you are reading this to move to a whole other level. There is a price to pay!

Are you on the right track? Ask yourself:

- How many three way validation and closing calls are you making?

- How many presentations per week are you attending or helping with? How many conference calls are you doing a week?

- How often are you at Saturday or Sunday Training?

- How much time are you spending giving of your best to others, regardless of downline affiliation or the Compensation Plan?

- How many times are you willing to travel, go to meetings and be stood up to find Success?

The next chapter will talk more specifically about the ingredients for a higher level of success.

4

Failing Your Way to the Top!

*T*he number one reason people do not join or quit so soon is Fear of Rejection! Why is that?

Most of us grew up being told:

- Don't do that!

- You can't have that!

- You can't do that!

- Or just plain: NO!

None of us likes to be told no. No one wants to feel rejected or turned down. No one wants to fail. However, one of the most important Success Lessons is that:

You cannot succeed your way to success!

You must fail your way to success!

You must learn to be willing to face rejection and failure over and over and embrace it as part of the learning process. After all, if you learn from failure it is not really failure. You have heard the clichés: *The Homerun King has more Strike Outs. The basketball star has missed more shots than he made*

27

and the Greatest Inventers fail over and over before they give us electricity, medicine, surgical procedures, technological advances all other great achievements.

Next, you have to realize that they are not really rejecting you but rather your product, service or opportunity. And frequently no does not mean no, it means not now or I don't have enough information. Don't take it so personal. After years in MLM I can tell you that you really can't say just the right thing to the wrong person.

Then you have to keep moving on.

> THE BIGGEST CHANGE IN MY MLM CAREER CAME WHEN I QUIT SPENDING TOO MUCH TIME WITH THE WRONG PEOPLE!

This is not for everyone. Let's face it. It is not for most. Sure everyone can do it but they won't! Sure you want it and feel it and perhaps you're even passionate about it but most people will say NO!

Regardless of how good you get at this:

- 80% of the people you ask will not even take a look.

- 50% of the ones that say they will look will not.

Only 50% of the ones that look will take the next step and join.

However, if you teach your Team to ask 2 or 3 a day it is a very manageable number for a part time person. That is at least 10 a week of which two people will say they will take a look and one will. Every two weeks you have a new Representative and if that goes through your downline, you are a raging success -- You have now Failed Your Way to Success!

5

Help Others Embrace Failure

*I*t is of extreme importance that you not only master dealing with rejection and failure for yourself but if you want a huge successful Team, you must teach it to all you come in contact with. I am a big fan of teaching the basics over and over. Really it is all about mastery of the basics so you can't hear it too many times. But understanding how to facing and deal with rejection is a very important basic.

There is a tendency in our industry to always talk about how great it can be and how simple it is and that is very true. However, we must also teach about reality. You already know the numbers so be sure to teach your new partners about it. I am not saying to talk negative at a presentation, just be positive about the realities of our business.

I like sayings like: "This is not for everyone". "What we do is not normal, but neither are the results", "Sometimes the lights are on but no one is home. Not everyone is going to get it". "However, there are millions of people out there hoping and praying for something just like this opportunity. Sharing this can not only change your financial life forever but thousands of other people's lives as well."

I have the rejection conversation at the first opportunity after someone registered. If they join at a meeting I immediately suggest that they not approach people about the opportunity until we have a planning and training session.

Forklift – If you owned a warehouse and just hired someone new you would not say, "hey if you are the first one there in the morning just jump on the fork lift and start moving things around. You will figure it out". For any business or job you must have a plan and start at the beginning. That is why we always have planning sessions.

Remind them that if they are coachable and teachable we can guide them about how to approach people and get the most positive results. And always remember this: "Asking Positive Questions Gets Positive Results".

Avoid negatives. **Talk about the positive side of almost everything** including problems. Yes, every problem is an opportunity! There are two kinds of people you do not want to work with; Lazy People and Negative People. There is almost never a cure for lazy and you don't even want to be around negative. I always remember the words of one of my greatest mentors, Chuck Hoover from Excel Communications. He said when people get negative to him he looks down at his feet and says, "Hey, I still have feet!" and then just walks away.

I have witnessed many people trying to change the mind of a negative person. I am not talking about someone that questions the business but someone that is truly negative. Not only does it not usually work, but if it does, you have just added a negative business partner. One bad apple …

So, it does not hurt to go over the statistics of rejection. After all, "The Truth Will Set You Free"! Don't dwell on it but make sure the new rep knows it is a normal part of the process. It takes a lot of "no's" to get to a "yes". It is just another law. Live with it and build your business.

Now, let's talk about fear of failure. For us it is important to know that many do not join because they just don' t believe they can be successful and most don't start things they may fail. If you can't run, you don't enter races. If you can't sing well, we all wish you wouldn't. You can succeed at Relationship Marketing so long as you follow the system. Some succeed very quickly and others take longer. However, I have met a lot of people that stuck with it for 10 or more years and found very rewarding success. Why not you?

After someone faces their fear and with your reassurance of help join, the risk of quitting goes off the charts as they will tend to return to their fear of failure. First, do it with them when they first start and you have greatly shielded them from failure. Or at least, you can share the hurt so it does not put them out of business. Then be aware that the fear of failure will continue to return at every hint of a roadblock.

"Be Big and Bold and Great and Mighty Forces Will Come to Your Aid!" You can make excuses or you can make money. You can't do both! Because of where my home is I cannot even be a customer of my company. I accepted the challenge and now even though I am not a customer I am paid on hundreds of thousands of them. There are very few challenges that do not carry with them a huge opportunity. There is a heads and tails on each coin. Just keep flipping!

In conclusion, we all deal with fear every day, especially fear of failure. You have to not only control your fear but help others do the same.

6

Steps to Higher Success

The Law of Large Numbers

We have all heard the law of large numbers but many spend all of their time breaking or trying to evade the law. It is a law. It may be fudged with luck or circumstance, but it will again take over. Let's talk about numbers.

As we discussed in the previous chapter, we must run a lot of numbers in recruiting in order to have success. Fortunately, many eventually understand and abide by this or they just don't make it. But if you want more than making it you must obey the inner laws.

> ***You Can Make Excuses or You Can Make Money. You Can't Do Both!***

Just as only 20% will ever look, of the ones that join, only about 10 to 20% will do very much. In itself, this is not a bad thing and is normal in virtually all areas of life. Many join churches but it is the few that make them work. Many start higher education but only a few receive higher degrees or more importantly use their education to improve our world, or even their own. As Jim Rohm would say, "It is just one of those things. You can't change it so live with it and stay focused on what you can change, yourself!"

In this book we are concerned with the inner or continuing laws that must be followed to climb to a very high level of Success. The simple answer is that the Law of Large Numbers continues at every level.

As your team begins to build, you must stay true to the law and realize that many join and only a few keep producing. However, it is frequently the ones that don't that bring in the ones that do. How is that you ask? Many times it is the 'sometimes rep' that brings in the 'mediocre rep', that in turn brings in another steadily building a whole team of 'mediocre reps'. Every once in a while even a blind squirrel finds a nut and it is one of our 'mediocre reps' that brings in the next Queen of Network Marketing! However, these members deserve your group time, not your personal time.

Again, the greatest change in my career came when I finally quit spending too much time with the wrong people. You know who they are: your friend that you want it for way more than they want it, your potentially strong prospect or rep that just does not get it or is not coachable, or the many that are in and want your time but are not doing the work to deserve your time.

Most good companies like mine, have a great back office that allows you to track all activities and most importantly separate fact from fiction. You have to constantly monitor to see who is really producing. Our goal is to run with runners all we can, walk with walkers when you have the time but never sit on the bench with anyone! Each day you must be identifying and reaching out to help and mentor those showing leadership potential. If you build leadership on your Team, all of the financial success will follow.

The 72 Hour Rule:

I use the 72 hour rule. Consultants that do something at least every 72 hours deserve your time. If a new consultant comes in and gets their first customers and consultants in the first few days, they deserve your help. If they promote and immediately recruit again, they are leaders in the making. Conversely, if they promote and spend the next days, weeks or months in Parade Mode – where they show up to be recognized for their previous success but do not bring guests or recruit new members -- the have stalled and may be done as a leader.

Let's stop to talk about that. All but the very best leaders will reach a certain level and stop. I don't mean take a break, but stop the very action that got them promoted. They will instead switch to management mode and hope for the downline to grow it for them.

As we all know, you must lead from the front so when you stop working, when you stop recruiting, bringing guest to presentations, stop gathering customers and looking for new leaders, your Team will mostly follow your lead and your growth has ended. Maybe that is all you want from your business.

If you build leadership on your team, all of the financial success will follow.

A great leadership practice is to call and congratulate people when they promote. People will frequently do more for recognition than they will for money; just give your recognition where it will do the most good. Just a quick call to congratulate them and remind them that now, more than ever is the time to recruit and build. Now is their chance to earn even greater income and reach closer to Financial Freedom. Watch your reports if you do. Many will take action, right after your call!

Again, I am not saying don't help the sometimes consultant, just help them in your group time not your personal time.

The most important ingredient in working toward success is merely to take massive action right away and consistently. A Great Best Seller on the subject is one of my favorites and helped many of my Team as well as myself. I highly recommend "Take Action Now" by Evan Money.

Evan has a very straightforward action plan for doing it now! There is no reason to spend an enormous amount of time planning and plotting. Once you have your goals it is more important to have an Action Plan and go for it. All of the knowledge in the world will not make you financially successful. It is only Massive Action that will dramatically improve your life.

The most important thing you can do is to take action now and every day toward your goals.

7

Building For the Next Event

*C*heck out any expert in MLM and they will talk about building for the next event. I call that a clue. Events are what builds belief and strengthens a consultant's belief to help bring about success. Every event has an impact on the growth of your business and that of your company. In my company, the largest event is the National Convention (We are only in a few states as of this writing). More than a third of our annual production comes in the two or three months following that event. What does not come in from that event is extremely influenced by that event and other events that build toward it. That is true of every Network Marketing Company. If you don't get that, you won't get it!

I am not a convention person. I come from the Insurance Industry and I dreaded every meeting and convention. I am a self-motivated, action-oriented guy. However, I learned that most people are not that way. Most people can't wait for the next event and it is the highlight of all they do. Once I learned this, it became the driver of my business as well. MLM is not about you! It is about helping others and if you want to be successful you had better center your business on building for the next event.

The next event is the next event. All year long we talk about the major event that is coming but as leaders we focus on having many small events, leading to larger events, leading to the big event, which leads to **big success**! Yet only about 5% of the representatives of any given company will show up for the largest of all events. Why? They don't know what you now know!

Human nature is to band together. Everyone loves a winner and events are a gathering of winners and those that want to win. Life is a blessing, but life is tough. No one of us can accomplish that much alone. But when we band together as a Team, we can move mountains! That is the nature of a well-planned event. Attending events will take you far but instigating and orchestrating them will take you over the top!

Most people will do far more for recognition than they will for money!

No one has ever built a large, fast growing, dynamic and exciting business without utilizing large exciting group presentations. One on one presentations are important. Two on one presentations lead to success. Home meetings, especially to launch a new consultant's business are an integral part of success. When done right, all of those tools lead to the Large Group, Corporate Overview often referred to as an Opportunity Presentation.

At each gathering and at the end of each conversation and presentation/training, we are talking about the next event. It is hard to stay on track if there is no target. The next event serves as the next target. We want to be talking to and about who can reach the next promotion level or sales quota by the next event so they will be recognized for their achievement at the event. Never forget: **Most people will do far more for recognition than they will for money!**

For some that may not make sense but understand that it is one of the laws of human behavior and whether you agree with it or not will not change it. Make sure recognition is a part of every gathering and every conversation for that matter. It is the Great Motivator!

When your company sets up events, be a leader at that event. Volunteer, purchase tickets early, perhaps even pre-purchase tickets for your Team. Show yourself to be an event supporter and you will find yourself in an Event Leadership Position. Do not segregate into Team Groups at Company Events. You are all on one Company Team at Company events. It builds solidarity and company-wide leadership cooperation. However, you do want to try and work in some Team time.

Look closely at the itinerary for upcoming company events and see if there is some down time from the company's itinerary so you and your Team can do something special. It can be as small as a reception, happy hour, leadership dinner or a major rally, but make sure it does not take away from the main event. Many use team shirts or colors to show their Team Pride at Company Events but know that when you do you walk a fine line between Team Pride and being Exclusive rather than Inclusive. If you want something to identify your Team I prefer a small lapel pin or something of that nature. You can see it when you look but it does not brag.

Insist on attendance. No, I don't mean you should force people to go to events, you should not even try. However, you are in charge of your private time and since we know those who attend events do the best in the business and we know we should spend more of our time with those that deserve our attention, it just stands to reason that you spend most of your private time with those that support and attend Group Events, Presentations and Trainings. It is the simple identifier.

Teach your folks that whenever possible, they should sit as close to the front as possible. People that sit in front see and are seen more, hear more and learn more. **That is why it is said, "All of the money is made in the front of the room".** It is just as important to be early, go in the room rather than gather in the hallways and never stand in the back!

At the first opportunity after a major event it is important to send out a re-cap and host Conference Calls, Webinars and Live Events to reinforce what came from the event. And of course, start talking and building for the next event.

8

Using Social Media

I am no expert in the use of Social Media. There are many great books out there but one of my favorites is from a real Networker, Wes Melcher called "Net-Easy-Marketing". I don't know that what we do qualifies as easy, but he explains very well how to use the cutting edge tools of our time to get the most out of your business. What I do know is that the same, tried and true rules, apply.

Don't use Facebook, Twitter and etc. to try and sell. Use them to build your brand and more importantly, to build your network. Again, this is Relationship Marketing and the relationship comes first. Social Media allows us to build relationships like never before. There are virtually no old friends that you can't find with a little clicking on the web and new friends are just a comment, photo or posting away. But don't think it is all-just for amusement.

Some of the fastest growing, largest companies in the world now rely on word of mouth advertising and much of it is driven by social media. It is one of the biggest changes in MLM in 50 years. Great conversations and meeting new, like-minded people is no longer geographically limited. But don't abuse it or you will be just as out as the abusive kid in grade school. And when you are un-friended in Facebook, you can't make up later on the playground.

If you use your Social Media to only post ads or worse, solicit new MLM Members or Customers, they will turn you off just like the commercials of old. TiVo was successful because people do not like to be inundated with commercials. But there are millions out there looking to make new friends, share common dreams and goals and how a happy fulfilled life can be achieved. And, people like to have fun!

Again, as I am not an expert I will not endeavor to tell you what to do but I will suggest that you post frequently, but not too frequently. Share success but don't brag. Post pictures of things that bring joy but never the opposite. And most of all, look, listen, learn and make friends.

> *MLM is not about you! It is about helping others.*

I love posting pictures of places I go and friends doing great things and I love when other people post positive things from my life. I always remember what a great athlete once said: "When you think you are good you feel like you have to talk about yourself. When you are great, others talk about you!" Remember that when you are tempted to brag on yourself and focus on the achievements of others instead. Never sell on Social Media!

Let's be clear. If you are posting recruiting messages and customer gathering messages you have broken the rule of success in not only Social Media, but also the Relationship Marketing Industry. People will no longer follow your postings or just un-friend you entirely. I sometimes have been criticized because there is too much related to my business on Facebook but as most of my life is related to my business, it is just natural. But I try to stay aware of it. And those embarrassing photos from the party, ball game or etc. just don't belong on Social Media. If you have the least concern about how it might make someone feel, don't post it.

9

Money Management

*Y*our goal is to not only earn a lot of money but to keep a great deal of it. Frequently in the long run, it will be more about what you save rather than how much you made. And too often I have seen seemingly successful representatives derailed because they did not plan for expenses and taxation.

I use a simple guideline. Of every dollar earned:

1. Set aside 35% for Taxes (The current top rate).

   You may not end up paying all of the taxes because of the write off benefits of our business and what is left can go to your savings.

2. Set aside 25% for savings. Pay your future first.

3. Live on 40%. Yes you can! We should all be starting this business part time and staying part time until you are making more than double from MLM what you were making in your traditional career or job.

Let's talk more about the 40%. In the beginning it will not be much but it is important that you train yourself well. Becoming wealthy involves on the job training. Mistakes are costly. It is much easier to learn before you are making really big money. And as your income goes up, you may need to adjust that percentage **down**! That's right, down.

Let's look at some real numbers:

- When you are earning $1000 a month
  o For Tax = $350
  o For Savings = $250
  o For Spending = $400

- When you earn $5000 monthly
  o For Tax = $1750
  o For Savings = $1250
  o For Spending = $2000

- When you earn $25,000 monthly
  o For Tax = $8750
  o For Savings = $6250
  o For Spending = $10,000

- When you earn $100,000 a month (That is why you are reading this, correct?)
  o For Tax = $35,000

- o For Savings = $25,000

- o For Spending = $40,000

Now it is time to raise the savings portion. I recommend shooting for 50% savings. When you put away over 50K a month, your savings dreams become a reality quickly. It will also make you feel safer with large investments.

> This is very important: People that plan to save later usually do not develop the habit and end up with insufficient or no savings at all. A person that earns a million and spends a million is BROKE! There will come a time for wonderful toys, vacations and even yachts and planes. However it is having substantial savings that will make it possible to do so without endangering everything you worked so hard for.

Learn to ask yourself; How will this expense or investment affect your future asset value? This is a line of thinking that one must constantly be using in order to become and stay wealthy. For most of us there is no practice or life guidance system on how to become and stay wealthy. If your parents were not wealthy they probably did not or could not teach you.

One of the best books on the subject is a favorite of mine and I recommend it often. Spend some time reading "How Rich People Think" by Steve Siebold. From his research, he explains the difference between the thinking of the middle class from that of the wealthy.

I am a fanatical accounting record keeper. The daily use of a program like Quicken will not only help you with the requirements of tax planning and expense management but also with planning. While I do use a great accountant and always have, I use a hands-on approach to income and expense management. Personal daily involvement with accounting keeps it not only on your mind but sharpens your ability to know where you are financially at all times. **Good decisions require good information.**

While I agree that one must spend money to make more money, each expense must make sense. I always make sure the expense makes sense in working toward my goals. I do not spend thousands, to make hundreds. Travel is a good example.

When my business was earning only a few thousand a month, I operated accordingly. I did not use air travel and expensive hotels when the activity I was traveling for could not justify the expense. When a trip to work another market was producing only a few hundred dollars a trip, I drove my car and stayed in modest motels. When it made sense to fly and rent cars it was because it gave me more time to work more market places and each trip could more than pay its own way.

My hotels got a bit nicer as a reward for my production becoming much higher. It does not work the other way around. To this day, I save my expensive hotels and resorts for vacation time when I can really get the value from the stay. Even as a Multi-Million Dollar Earner, my business hotels are Marriott, Sheraton, Doubletree and other 3-4 Star Hotels. I want a safe, clean and restful sleep and work place at a good price. Not being wasteful is a good trait that adds to your savings and financial future.

While I probably flew coach too long, it was important to me to control costs. I saved as much as possible on every flight which added to my saving toward private aviation.

I ask that my major purchases add to the value of my business. After reaching a seven figure annual income I moved to a high end Tour Bus. It not only allowed me to take huge advantage of travel time (While a professional driver drove, I wrote, planned and made calls). It also allowed me to show thousands of people the dream that hard work and success in MLM provided. Thousands of people were exposed to Bigger Thinking by visiting me in my Tour Bus in literally hundreds of Hotel and Meeting Room Parking Lots. Again, making sure that the expense added value to the growth of my business. Eventually, I just required a faster way.

I am known for making more personal appearances in more places. I travel frequently speaking, training and helping develop leaders. That kind of travel takes a toll on you over the years and as the income and productiveness made sense, I bought my own plane.

Charter is a great way to go. However, since I far exceed the minimum threshold of 150 hours flight time per year I found more value in ownership. I use two types of ownership. I own a conservative but very nice late model turboprop airplane that research showed is in great demand for business charter. I put my plane with a management company and it is dry leased to other users when I am not using it. Some months my airplane even more than pays for itself, while always helping to reduce the expenses. As long as you can afford to pay for the plane and all expenses, even without the lease or charter income, it can be a very effective use of money.

As it is not cost effective to use my plane on very long trips where there will be a lot of non-flying time, I fly commercial across the country and then use fractional ownership for my local or regional travel. I own part of a late model piston commuter plane that is in a sharing program. The management company takes care of the plane and the logistics and I reserve and use it to again do more presentations and trainings in more places without the hours lost and hassle of commercial flight. It also eliminates much of the time and trouble of packing and unpacking, as I am able to stay in a central location or hub, while making daily flights to increase productivity.

Both of my planes take the Dream Showing to a whole new level. I always try to have local leaders pick me up from private FBO Flight Facilities allowing for photo time and sharing of the dream. Those leaders not only have their vision stretched, they share the experience with others. It is often said that if you fly in people think more of your expertise. When it is on your own plane it raises the level even more. And, every chance I get I take one or two leaders or prospects along with me on the flights.

I combine working toward my dreams with living my dreams. Rather than retire and live off the few years of hard work (And that is certainly a possibility), I choose to take my dreams and put them to work. This year I purchased an 80-foot Hargrave Custom Motor Yacht. It is in a class known as Super Yachts as it is still smaller and more personal than a Mega-Yacht but loaded with luxury. Many of my days are spent working from, cruising or relaxing on my yacht while flying off in the evening to do even more meetings. Whenever possible I invite leaders along for the cruise or just back to visit the boat.

I have a Facebook page just for my yacht and the travels. It helps thousand that may not visit the yacht in person participate in the dream. I have Hargrave manage the boat advising me all the way, sharing their years of experience while also leasing the yacht out for well-chosen charters when I am not using it. Again, they not only save me money while protecting the yacht's future value, they actually help bring in income to offset the expense. Again though, make sure you can afford the monthly expenses without charter income before you even consider ownership. By the way, many of the top people at Hargrave Custom Yachts including the owner, Michael Joyce and my personal Yacht Broker, Herman Pundt along with many others are also participating in my MLM Business. It is not just a token; they see the value in what I do as well. Even the broker for the seller, Gibbs Lukoskie, joined my team and is having great success.

Close your eyes for a moment and think about the future that is available to you. In just a few short years you could go from driving daily to work your business while staying in very modest hotels to flying home from a great training/presentation on your own plane taking you back to the Master Stateroom of a Multi-Million Dollar Luxury Yacht. Will it happen for you? I don't know that, I only know that it could.

Don't want to do the accounting? Rather spend money now and worry about the future later? **Rather live extravagantly now, or plan for a Dream Life? You choose.**

10

Time Management

*N*ow would be a good spot to talk about Time Management. First, to again quote John Maxwell: "You really can't manage time." We all have the same amount of time. However, we can manage ourselves, and what we do with our time. I am going to talk about several aspects of Time Management that will directly affect your future success.

> *To be successful, you have to take massive action, every day!*

Hopefully you learned in the early chapters to set a specific time aside for personal growth. That is very important to your Success. But let's talk about the value measurement of your time.

The evening hours from 5 p.m. until 9 p.m. are the most valuable hours in your day. Those are the hours that are easily worth hundreds if not thousand of dollars per hour to you. Be very careful how you spend them. What does it really cost you to watch TV from 7 p.m. to 9 p.m. on a Thursday? Quite possible the compound value of that is a fortune.

Before you choose an activity or place it on your calendar you should assign a value to it. Don't let yourself get caught up in $10 and hour work during $100 an hour time. Need to get organized, do it in the morning or late night. Need to make congratulatory phone calls, do them in the daytime. Need to update your Facebook or Twitter? Do that late at night or early in the morning when you can't be talking to a prospect, consultant or presenting your business opportunity.

Work from a calendar. Think about where you put or do certain activities and don't get lost in the process. To be successful, you have to take massive action, every day! To get the best results, you must pick the time for your action. Work can't be both convenient and highly productive. You have to give up some things to someday get all you ever dreamed of.

How you spend [your time] will not only determine your success but the success of all that follow you.

The second aspect of time management is when do you give your time and how much of it. We already talked about how to determine who deserves it and now it is time to make your blueprint.

Early in your career, when you have not been promoted it is all about recruiting and gathering customers. Do not spend more than 10% of your time managing even the people you bring in. You are part of a team with a hierarchy of leadership. Follow the system. Most of the true help for your new recruits should come from the more experienced upline. It just makes sense for them to learn from the best and any decent compensation plan is set up with this in mind.

Years ago I began volunteer work as an EMT. It was early in the development of the advanced Emergency Medical Care System and most EMS Services were still provided by funeral homes etc. Their system was simple. The most experienced person drove the ambulance while the new person attended to the patient. It is hard to understand how that ever made sense, but it certainly was not good for the survival rate. Don't use a similar system for your Network Marketing System.

Sure, you should be helping them make invitations and ask for customers but deliver them to your experienced upline for 3 way calls, training and coaching. It means far more that you go with your new consultants to training rather than try to teach them yourself. We should all learn from as close as possible to the master. Our skills are handed down from leader to leader but only perfected with field experience. Trust only in Successful, Experienced Leaders to train you and your Team.

As you climb the Promotion Stairway of Success, you will add more time for management as you assume more of the leadership, but only as you have shown field success. To do so early is a mark of probable ego restrictions. While a certain amount of strong ego is one of the keys to success, one must control it all of the time. No matter how much you know, there is always someone you can learn from that knows more.

Here is a good chart:

Beginner:	**90% Recruiting**	**10% Management**
Lower Levels	**70% Recruiting**	**30% Management**
Middle Levels	**60% Recruiting**	**40% Management**
Top Levels	**40% Recruiting**	**60% Management**
The Top	**20% Recruiting**	**80% Management**

*****

One should always have three personally recruited consultants that deserve their time. You have to recruit more than that as we learned earlier. So, since two are probably looking for a place to stop you had better have a few more started and some in the funnel.

Never stop recruiting. It is not a start and stop process but an ongoing daily process. When you stop recruiting, you stop growing.

Although you work with individuals, you should think in Teams. It takes very large Teams to be very Successful. Let's start thinking in legs. Legs are a common MLM Term and refer to all of the people under a personally sponsored rep. It may start with the person you sponsored or it may be whoever really started the growth on that leg. Frequently the best leaders occur deep in your downline under a string of average business builders. Look for and identify these legs or Team Leaders.

Until you reach the highest level you should always be dividing your time between 3 or 4 legs and your recruiting time. So in the Middle Level above, it would be 10% of your time with each of your 3 hot legs and 10% with all of the others while your recruiting time may be 10% with each of 4 and 20% on personal recruiting.

Make a chart that fits your organization. Have a plan and work your plan. Don't allow luck or an accident to control your growth. I have been very lucky at MLM. As a matter of fact, the harder I work the luckier I get, but it is not haphazard.

All great businesses have a business plan. Yours can be quite simple but you must know how much time you are going to spend each day, and what you are going to spend that time on. Your time is the most valuable asset or currency you have. How you spend it will not only determine your success but the success of all that follow you. **Don't waste your valuable time on frivolous or menial activities.**

I have spent 19 years developing my skills and habits as a network marketer and over 30 years in traditional business. I have seen many reach their goals even more quickly than me but I always knew mine were coming. It may sound cold at first, but **be very careful of your time and how you spend it!**

11

Colors of Success

*H*ave you ever wished you could just look at someone and know his or her personality? Wouldn't it be great if people came with labels so you could know right away what kind of things are important to them? While I can't make that happen, I can share a system that with practice can help you very quickly identify a person's personality and more importantly let you know how to relate to them.

> *You have to give up some things to someday get all you ever dreamed of.*

This system is taught by many different trainers with variations as frequent as the number of trainers. While I have heard it many times the one that made the most sense to me and helped me put it into practice was from Renowned Trainer, Marc Accetta. It is of course altered by my years of personal experience.

First it is important to know that pretty much all people have some of all four traits that we categorize and label with colors. What differs, is what they have the most of and what drives them to their decisions and actions. While you are reading this you should start to identify each of these personality colors as they exist and or dominate you. Marc has some great tests to help you figure out where you are but you can pretty much get there with some objective examination.

Blue People

The first color we talk about is also the most prevalent. More people are dominated by the personality color blue than all others. Because of this, it is very important that we prepare to communicate with the "Blue People".

Blue People tend to focus on having a good time. They think about and are driven by having fun! It can be great in the Blue World as the driving factors are not really facts, figures and numbers. They don't really want to study all of that stuff and as long as your compensation plan pays out a lot of money, that is pretty much all they need to know about the details.

Blue People are more interested in having a good time, being social and enjoying life. When communicating with and recruiting a Blue Person it is imperative that you not wear them out with too many details. You have to be sure and talk about all the fun we have, the simplicity, how much it just makes sense and how we can have a good time while making a lot of money which is also, a lot of fun!

Remember, blue is the most frequently dominating color so your pitch about facts and figures will quickly cause them to tune you out and daydream about fun stuff!

A presentation or training event full of Blue People is a great event. Emotions run high, people have fun and having a lot of Blue People attracts even more Blues and it is the largest group!

Green People

Green is a very solid trait that is easily identified. Usually you can spot a Green Person by his or her occupation. They thrive on numbers, facts and figures. They lean toward Accounting,

Engineering, Banking and other fields where it is important to be precise. Sure they like to have fun but they think facts and figures are fun!

You have to be precise to hold the attention of a Green Person. You are better off giving them a copy of your compensation plan because they are not interested until they know it well. You can't spout approximates or especially false facts and figures or they will discount everything you say after you do. Be as detailed as possible but don't be afraid to defer to their ability and merely offer to give them the book, the kit or other detailed information so they can get the facts and figures. These are very powerful allies but you won't woo them with empty presentations centered on emotion -- they want facts!

There is a bonus here, Green People will help you and your team stay organized. They will help you become accountable and give you back more details than you ever had before, so you can recruit even more Green People.

Yellow People

These are some of the best. Yellow People care more about how others feel than they do money, facts, figures, fun or even themselves. Yellow people are always interested in your family and will not be a part of something that does not strive to make it better for all.

Yellow People worry more about the way others feel than they do the compensation plan. They want to make sure everything is inclusive, not exclusive. They definitely don't care how much you know until they know how much you care.

There are less Yellow People than any of the other colors. However, they are crucial to the survival of your team. They are constantly looking out for the mental and emotional as well as physical well being of others. Sprinkle some Yellow in your team and you will be much closer to being a family.

Yellow People hardly ever offend anyone. They are careful about the feelings of others and will help you grow a team that sticks together. I try all the time to grow in my Yellow Trait.

Red People

This is a tough group. Red personality types are very driven and like to be in charge. Red People like control and will compete to be the leader. Red People can frequently hurt the feelings of others and sometimes turn off or offend others. However, they usually are the leaders. Someone has to lead and Red People are glad to step up.

Red People like to hear how they can make huge sums of money and how they can lead so many others. They love to be loved and will work hard for respect and admiration. They may forget your children's names or maybe even yours, but you can follow them to success. Red would rather go through an obstacle rather than loose the time going around and **they don't wait!**

Patience is not a virtue in Red People. However, they are great for high speed and high activity levels and for facing a deadline and getting it done. The speed of the leader is usually the speed of the pack so recruit some Red People and they will raise the pace of the whole team.

How do we put all of this to use?

Know that all people have some of all of the colors, but learn to listen early for the signs of these colors in a person. As you begin to recognize the colors you will be able to adjust your content and delivery. You will learn their personality and then customize your invitation to make them more apt to take a look at your presentation.

If you are to be a truly effective public speaker, you must include a little for each of these personality traits in every presentation and training. With a little practice you will include a message for each of these groups in every large presentation and customize your individual presentations to fit the prospect.

If all you talk about is money to a Yellow, they are not going to join you. If you hammer Blues with facts, figures and details they will tune you out. If you talk only emotion or give wrong details to a Green they will probably write you off. If you neglect to tell Reds that they can be in charge and change the world while earning a fortune, as others look on with great admiration, you may loose a lot of potentially great leaders.

Make it a game to learn and practice reading people. Not just in your MLM Business but in life. You will be surprised not only how quickly you become adapt at this but how soon it begins to change your business.

...I am a Red/Green/Blue/Yellow.

Red dominates many of my decisions and certainly my work ethic. I strive to temper my Red with the other colors while maintaining the strength of a Red.

I have a lot of Green. Early in life I excelled at accounting and math and thought I would be an engineer. Facts, Figures and the Compensation Plans are very important to me and I read and study information all the time. It is my Green that drives me to get the information that helps me recruit Green People.

I am a little weaker at Blue. I love people and I love to have fun, but my serious side frequently wins out. I will not often sacrifice success for fun but when I can do both I am very happy.

As I said I am weakest at Yellow. So, I not only work on that all the time but I work to recruit and attract more Yellow People to help me and my team take good care of others.

My previous MLM Company was founded and run by two Blue guys. They were great Networkers and focused so much on having fun that they started a company whose motto was "Making a Living, Living". They were both 6 figures a month earners before they started their own company and have gone on to build a very successful company. They are pros and have surrounded themselves with Green, Red, Yellow and other Blues. Blue is generally the largest group.

No matter how much you know, there is always someone you can learn from that knows more.

Executive Consultant Greg Henzel is in his first MLM opportunity. He has always been an entrepreneur as evidenced by his background as the owner of Jewelry Stores and Smoothie Shops. You can see his aggressive Red Characteristics, while his Green Side keeps all of the numbers straight. He truly cares about everyone, which is the best of Yellow Traits, but he is led by Blue!

Greg always makes uplifting comments and it is as fun to hear him speak as it is just to hang out with him. He attracts and gets along with everyone, shows them a good time while becoming one of the Top Leaders in the Industry. Like Greg, most Blue People have a lot of friends and everyone they meet joins that group!

My good friend Dr. Thomas O'Grady is one of those Ultra-Green

People. Yes, he is Red enough to be an achiever, yet Yellow enough to care about others. Like all Blues he loves to have a good time but, he is lead by Green. Thomas has a PH.D. in Economics and had an outstanding career as a consultant to many large companies before embarking on Network Marketing. He kept the facts, figures and details straight and has reached the highest levels in MLM with a huge team. He is now known at the MLM Doc!

Red is present in all leaders and many of them manage to control the Red and use it to reach the highest levels. My good friends Damien Pechacek and Shawn Cornett are the longtime partnership of a Red/Blue/Yellow/Green working with a Red/Green/Blue/Yellow to build a Million Dollar MLM Team. I have known them for years and they always reach the higher levels of what they do. Being driven drives them. They do their very best even when no one else is watching because they are watching!

Yellow may not be the dominant trait often but I have watched as my good friend Pastor Kenny Smith consistently leads with his concern for others. Having reached the highest levels of success in MLM he is still active as a Pastor. He likes to tease that he is the only Top Leader that does not ever want to fire his boss!

Kenny wants more for his family and loves to have a great time but will not sacrifice that special Yellow Quality of truly caring for others. He and many other pastors, ministers, rabbis, priests and other religious leaders find great success in the Network Marketing Industry not only because of the other great qualities but also because they posses the developed Yellow personality of always caring.

From the first time I heard this concept, it became one of my life's pursuits. I love studying people and learning to communicate with them with a message and its delivery, which is acceptable and even desirable to them. I constantly strive to appeal to and be aware of all of the colors in my public speaking. I guess it is part of being a Red/Green/Blue/Yellow.

12

Focus on Building Leadership

*T*here is nothing more important to your success than building leadership. If your team does not have a large number of leaders it will turn upside down and the weight of trying to help so many people will crush your business. So many let their ego get in the way as they want to be the "Big Leader" and they do all they can to build followers rather than leaders. While it is true that you have to be a good follower before you can be a good leader, if you don't take the next step and allow or even push your team to become leaders, you are in trouble.

Now leading leaders is very rewarding and very difficult at the same time. I have heard it compared to herding cats, as they all tend to go their own direction. It's ok! Let leaders learn to lead. If you lead from the front, do more, work harder and thus have more success, they will follow. However, there are two kinds of leaders.

Many leaders are really commanders. They lead like a general or a coach giving orders to their troops or players and rendering punishment when they don't do as commanded. While I have seen leaders build big teams and make a lot of money doing just that, it is a very stressful, angry and resentful existence that is usually short term as well. If you find yourself always telling people what to do, you should examine your motives and make sure your team really does come first.

Then there are true leaders. They lead from the front more like the lieutenant or quarterback rather than the general or coach. They never ask people to do what they haven't and usually lead the way.

People tend to follow them out of choice rather than fear. They truly love others and usually get that love in return.

True leaders are frequently surprised by their own success as they were so focused on the success of others that they did not even see it coming.

When you understand the difference and choose true leadership your life will be greatly improved, your stress and aggravation lessoned and you will exceed even your goals.

It is often said that Network Marketing is a Personal Development Program with a Compensation Plan attached. That has been true in my life. The more I worked and studied to improve myself, to become a better leader and thus more valuable, the more money came my way.

There is nothing more important to your success than building leadership.

My good friend Chris Atkinson was down and out when we met. He was afraid of public speaking and had no interest in trying to lead anyone, even himself. He became a student of MLM and the Personal Development that comes with it. He went from broke to making a few thousand dollars a month. Then Chris really stepped up and pushed himself to become a speaker, a Team Leader, a Leadership Development student and Teacher. His focus on becoming better at helping and more valuable to others has now made him one of the most sought after Passionate Public Speakers and Trainers and a Multi-Million Dollar Earner in MLM. Chris changed his focus from trying to make a living to trying to be a Better Leader. Not only has his life changed forever but he is changing the lives of others, daily.

In my early years working in the Network Marketing Industry I recruited using salesmanship and spent much of my time trying to drag people across the finish line. I had been a salesman much of my life and my main career was as an Insurance Agent. In that industry they teach closing, over and over. It is all about identifying or even suggesting a need and making the sale. I used the same technique and it seemed to work, but the team did not grow, as it could not duplicate much less multiply.

I was quickly known as a recruiter as I was able to get in front of people, one on one, and simply convince them that they needed to join my company. At first I was so busy selling that I did not even consider what the people I brought in would do. I thought they would all do the same thing as me. Boy was that a mistake. Remember, most people are not salespeople and frequently don't even like salespeople. My business was doomed from the start.

My idea of leadership was as a Sales Manager. I just continued to encourage people to sell, sell and sell. I pushed people to become salespeople and if they did not, I just sold to new people and repeated the process. It never even occurred to me that this was not just a business of selling. Although some sales techniques are helpful, if you convince people to join you have little chance of them engaging and going to work.

By the time I had recruited my first 20 or so people and had almost no production, I still did not get it. I simply switched my target market and began to recruit sales people. There is no telling how many sales people I influenced to do it all wrong and thus fail in MLM. I began to read; listen and study true leaders in MLM and personal development. I began to notice for the first time that the Top Earners with huge teams were usually not sales people. My slow turn to success started with that realization.

As I said, I also pushed others and tried to pull people I cared about over the finish line to success. It sure got old dragging a bunch of people that just did not want to go. The biggest change in my career came when I simply quit spending so much time with the wrong people and learned that it was all about:

Ways to Focus on Building Leadership

1. Make a list

2. Invite, Invite and Invite

3. Expose people to the business

4. Follow up and register ONLY THE ONES THAT GOT IT!

5. Teach people to tell and not sell

6. Lead from the front by setting the correct example

7. Consistently make new friends and add to my list

8. Never Pre-Judge

9. Embrace Failures and learn from them

10. Spend time with those that deserve my help, not those that just want or need it!

11. Never forget that you may be just one person away from a life-changing breakthrough.

12. Focus your attention on the success of others, as the people you help develop leadership skills will determine your future.

Now, I am blessed with hundreds of leaders that continue to build leadership, and my team has a life of its own. I focus on identifying new leaders and reach out to them. I know that each time a new leader advances in leadership skills, our whole team and company rise. I do not spend much time talking about products, services or sales. I spend most of my time talking about learning more, helping more and from that process, getting closer to your dreams.

I encourage, but realistically. I like to talk to people about how their life can be if they focus on learning and helping more. Recently, as I finished a talk to a few hundred consultants and their guests, a 67 year old lady approached me with tears in her eyes. She said she drove quite a distance to attend the presentation as a last effort. She said that was the day she had decided to quit. To give up!

She held my hand and thanked me for talking openly about failure and how it is natural and the road to success. I had spoken about embracing failure, learning from it and moving closer to your dreams. She was touched that I was an ordinary guy and talked openly about the challenges but reinforced that "How you face those challenges will change your life".

She said her husband had retired years ago but that the downturn in the economy had diminished their 401k Pension Plan and that at 67 years of age he was back working the night shift at a plant. She shared that each morning when he came home he stopped, bought a fast food breakfast and brought it home to share with her. She smiled and said she was not quitting and would hold fast to her goal of bringing her husband home from work. She impacted my life in a very positive way as well. Moments like that mean more than money.

The biggest change in my career came when I simply quit spending so much time with the wrong people.

Each time we identify and help a new leader develop their leadership skills, a whole new team is built on our team. I have enjoyed seeing tens of thousands make enough extra money to buy a car, get a nicer family home, send their kids to better schools and just live a better life. I have seen hundreds develop their leadership skills and personal value to the level that they no longer work jobs or traditional business and have set themselves Financially Free to live their dreams!

How about you? Are a few minutes of personal development training, every day, worth it to live your dreams? The most powerful thing you can experience is to pursue personal development and become more valuable to yourself and others.

Through Personal Development Training you become more valuable. **As you become more valuable you attract more money.** You are compensated based on the value you bring to others.

13

Claiming Your Territory!

*M*any in MLM build a large team without ever leaving their home market. You simply continue to build a fire at home, recruiting and teaching them to recruit. Your Team will not only grow at home but all across the globe and your company's territory. However, if you want to make it to the extreme levels of financial success in MLM you must not wait, but go and claim your territory.

The most powerful thing you can experience is to pursue personal development and become more valuable to yourself and others.

Much of my current success came because I was willing to work consistently in many new markets. Work through the initial rush, the slowdown as the "Lottery Ticket Reps" go away and help the eventual real builders put the location on the map. You have heard it said; "If you will do what others won't, you will get what others don't". This law applies a great deal when it comes to expanding your footprint! However, don't just pack up and go hound the locals. That seldom produces anything good.

To open a new territory is simply using the all-governing law of relationship marketing. Everyone knows someone that knows someone that knows someone in the territory you desire. You must make a consistent effort to not only get those referrals but follow up on them as well. Every time you talk to anyone, downline, customers, prospects and suspects, you must be asking:

"Who do you know that might know someone that knows people in 'XYZ' town?

As we said in our previous book, "Of Course You Can", this is one of the most powerful tools you have while being the one most often missed. I did not really know anyone in New York and had only been there once but I asked everyone I spoke to who they knew. Does it work? I now count well over 30,000 on my team in New York and they have spread to many other states. I am glad I asked for referals. Are you asking?

When you get a referral, you need to pounce on it with a sense of urgency. Don't put it off. Every day you wait is another chance for them to end up on some other Team. Just ask: "Will you please introduce me to them, right now? They will sure be glad you did". Then call the person... yes, right now!

Introduce yourself to the prospect and tell them your purpose with excitement and a sense of urgency. Say something like: *"My name is Steve Thompson and I am spearheading the expansion of my company into your area and we are looking for sharp ambitious people. Do you know anyone that may like another stream of revenue because if you do, that person may be able to make a lot of money and gain market advantage?"*

Notice that I don't try and recruit them directly. I ask whom they might know. Regardless of what they say, they are frequently thinking "Yes, me!". It will just be easier to get there by making it second person.

Who put me in charge of "Spearheading Expansion"? I did! You better put yourself in charge and then put your new responsibility to work.

Once you have recruited a couple it is still not time to go there. Let me explain… Early in my career I traveled all over the country trying to help my new recruits and found it unproductive. Since I was doing it for them they never really learned. It never created a leader, just a dependent. Your system should be strong enough that they can get to at least their first promotion working with a local Team and your phone support. If they can't, they probably were not the right person and certainly not a leader. And again, what we are looking for are leaders.

Your business success is greatly determined by your network and the network of those that join your team.

Once they have a few on their team and have been promoted it is time to visit. Set a date a couple of weeks out and let them know. Teach them how to set up special meetings, lunches and dinners. Then go back to everyone you know and let them know you are about to go work with your team in 'XYZ City' and who do they know that might know some people there. There is no use in even having a trip if you are not going to promote it. So promote it to everyone. When you finally get there you will have significance and a larger number of people.

If you do get a team going somewhere else and go to visit, your main priority is to plug them in with the local Team. Do not separate them from local leadership and try to do it yourself. Plug them into the system.

Now, a word about sharing: The greatest success is gained by giving away your very best tools and skills. Your generosity will help others and in turn you will be rewarded. All ships rise in a high tide so let's help make the tide as high as possible. Never be selfish or secretive. Be open, honest and share your best. Keep your arms open to all.

When you are in a different town as a visiting leader, make sure to offer your help to any local meetings or trainings. It will make you a better leader and your Team will be much more welcome. If you go in, do your own thing and only work with your folks, you are creating animosity, selfishness and jealousy. Remember, there is more than enough for everyone.

More people turn 18 each year than have ever been in Network Marketing. There is no chance of saturation and no reason to think of scarcity. Focus on abundance and you will have it all. After all, you get what you focus on!

Some of my best friends and greatest business partners are people I met while following this system. Don't be afraid of new places and people. There is a huge upside as you not only spread the success, but also learn from so many different cultures. I specifically focus on different cultures.

Not only is there faster growth in immigrant cultures, there is much to learn from them. 1st and 2nd generation Americans are wonderful to work with and frequently have much larger networks of people that really stick together and watch out for each other. What a fantastic way to grow yourself while you grow your business.

Your business success is greatly determined by your network and the network of those that join your Team. Wouldn't it be nice to learn from and work with close-knit groups like people who stick together because of nationality, religion, occupation, personal beliefs or ways of life? **Be alert to opportunities but always seek to serve, not sell. If you truly focus on helping others they will help you.**

There is nothing much more rewarding than having people be grateful for your help while your company pays you thousands of dollars for that same action. I have earned millions by focusing on doing good things for other people. **The reward is more than monetary.**

14

Play Where the Money Is, But Don't Neglect Anyone

*W*hen you first begin a new Network Marketing business it is not necessary that you understand all of the intricacies of the Compensation Program. However, learning it fairly quickly is one of the keys to quicker success and less frustration from missteps. While most companies do a good job of illustrating their compensation programs they can still be a mystery to a novice.

Your best education is from training seminars and consultation with experienced representatives of that company. Making sure you are getting the right information and understanding it is your responsibility. Be sure to ask questions about what you don't understand and make sure the teacher has the success to back up his or her teaching. This is a great time to turn to Consultant Sponsored Websites like **www.AmbitPros.com.** They will offer the easiest-to-understand explanations of your compensation plan and how it compares to others. But remember, it is your responsibility.

I suggest that you never neglect to help a Team Member because of his placement in your compensation plan. There are several strong reasons for this. Let's discuss a couple of the big ones:

Each person in your business is connected to almost everyone else in your business some way at some time. Even if you do not receive strong compensation for helping a particular person (not Coded, Not in your pay leg and etc.), that person's activity and success will affect everyone they come in contact with. If one horse in a pack runs faster, even if that is not your horse, they all run faster. I have seen so many times in my career that when I help a person that I am not directly compensated for, he or she ends up leading people that are in my compensation. You also never know where life will lead you.

The person that reaches out to you for help may pay you in ways you can't see. I hope you chose the right company for yourself the very first time, but that did not happen for me. However, in my last company there were several people that I worked with personally that I was not compensated for at the time. Years later those same people either were on my Pay Line or they greatly influenced people that were.

I worked with a new friend, Chris Atkinson, in the travel industry. I could not get paid for Chris's Activity or that of his team. However, we not only talked almost daily, I frequently traveled to do presentations and trainings with him. People thought I was crazy! When I started with my current company, the greatest success of my life, Chris joined me and we worked together like never before. His personal growth has made the single largest impact on my growth and income. And he is only one great example of those that started as unpaid work and later became hugely financially rewarding.

Chris is now National Consultant Chris Atkinson and has built a Huge Team on my Team.

So, never neglect people. However, it is important to consistently play where the money is.

With the bulk of your personal time you should be recruiting and working with those that can and will pay you the most money (See the chapter on time management). The combination of a good understanding of the compensation plan along with placing the majority of your efforts accordingly, will yield great results.

I place a value on my time. There are times of day where I am the most valuable like recruiting, training, conference calls, 3 way calls and etc. There are also parts of my organization that are the most "Financially Valuable". You must pay attention to that and not yield to the easier, lower paying task of continuing to help the same people over and over again. It is always easier to only work with those that already know what they are doing, than it is helping develop new leaders that create massive success. There we go with that leadership thing again!

Learn the Compensation Plan and take charge of your own future and the results from your work. Make sure you are "Playing Where the Money Is" to get the greatest financial results.

15

Multiplication, Not Just Duplication

*E*veryone in MLM talks about the power of Duplication. The act of teaching someone to do what you just did in order to spawn a duplicate of you to gain leverage. It is not just very important but imperative if you are to grow your business with leverage. However, it is Multiplication that combines leverage with true geometric growth to create massive success. And, it is not really people that duplicate, it is the systems that duplicate.

Leaders throughout the industry agree that you can't really duplicate people although that phrase is used all the time. It is only through the use on Simplistic Systems that we ever have true Duplication. While you can't really duplicate a person, many people can duplicate the application of a simple, duplicable system.

First, take the personality out of it. If your personality, or that of a few others drives your business, it will not get far. People can't clone themselves and everyone has a skill set just a little bit different from everyone else. So duplication of personality driven success is short lived. You may find a few others sort of like you, but the process is slow and runs its course very quickly. If you have been in the industry for a while and seem to recruit very well but do not see much duplication in your team, then this is probably the culprit. I have sat with many initially successful consultants that hit a wall and yearned to know what was wrong. That's when I share my past experience with that same failure and suggest the newer leader start over with the system rather than their skillfulness or salesmanship.

Many companies have developed systems for recruiting, training and building teams. Generally, it may not come from the company but rather from field leadership. If you can't find the system in your company do some research talking with the biggest leaders and learning how they do it. Only if you can't find it should you try to create the system and then only by working with some successful system developers. They can be found in a search of Personal Development Trainers that come from a successful background in MLM. When my company started we brought together some top leaders with system experience and put together our system. Although we sometimes tweak the system, our focus is on Duplication, not Innovation.

It is multiplication that combines leverage with true geometric growth to create massive success.

The system must be simple and be based on duplicable recruiting scripts, videos, online presentations, 3 way calls and trainings that all follow the same system. It must never require the use of personally done presentations in a one on one or two on one setting. If your system uses flip charts or PowerPoint's for people to use on individual presentations, take them out! The only time you should use live, personal presentation is in a group setting. That could be a home meeting/grand opening party of 30 or more or a hotel/training center presentation of even more. Individual Presentations done at the inappropriate time will put an end to duplication.

It all goes back to keeping the personality out of the system. Personal Presentation requires the outgoing personality and speaking skill. Those two skills are not so frequent. While there will be people fighting over the chance to speak in front of groups, getting everyone on your team comfortable with live presentations just won't happen. And it does not need to!

While you may not close as many using a video as compared with personal presentation and selling skills, remember that signing people up is not the goal. Getting Team Members to engage in the use of a successfully duplicating system for success is! Trust the system approach. It will not only work, it is the only thing that will allow you the magic of Multiplication.

When one person teaches another how to show a video to a prospect you have duplication; when both of those individuals each show another you have four; when they each show a few, that show a few, that show a few, you have multiplied. Now hundreds if not thousands are working the system simultaneously. Stick to the system. It may take a little longer to get it going but you may find that you end up with a system that continues to work so you don't have to. This is the simple key to massive growth in your MLM Business.

One of the largest crippling mistakes in MLM is to sell the opportunity to people through personal presentation and sales skills. If you have to talk them into your business, you will have to talk them into doing anything. The goal is not to sign people up but rather to find excited, motivated people and help them engage!

Showing the business personally in one-on-one presentations by flip chart or even PowerPoint defeats any chance of multiplication. Don't fall into the trap of making this a personality driven sales business. You don't want a job; you want a business, one that works even when you don't!

Congratulations to You!

You are already a **hero** of your own Personal Development! Many people will start this or other books and never get this far. Just by getting to this little note you have proven yourself to truly be on a quest for success.

Although it is often said that knowledge is power, that is just not true. It is the application of that knowledge that will bring you power. However, by becoming a student of Personal Development and becoming a student that completes the study, you are more prepared for that Massive Activity that will bring you success.

My personal congratulations to you!

To Success,

Steve

16

Perfect Practice

*T*here are but a few skills that you must master to be very successful in this business. You don't have to be a great presenter (But being in front of the room lends you tremendous credibility). You don't have to be a great closer as long as you remember to use 3 way calls when recruiting by phone and put your prospects in front of leaders/closers at live presentations. You don't even have to know that much about your compensation or marketing plan. What you do have to get good at is the Invitation, the 3 Way Call and Follow Up.

A great inviter goes to the top. It is a numbers game and all of the skills in the world won't make up for talking to enough people. It is often said that you can't say enough of the right things to the wrong person and you really can't say enough of the wrong things to the right person. You just have to find the right person!

Get with the successful people on your team and learn the word track they use to invite people to take a look. Put it in your own words and practice it. **While it is often said that Practice makes Perfect, it is really only Perfect Practice That Makes Perfect.** So develop or obtain the invitation script or scripts, review them for accuracy with successful leaders and then practice them with a friend, or even in front of the mirror. Make sure you are held accountable and that you practice like your business depends on it…because, it does!

Remember that the invitation is just that, an invitation. Don't try to tell someone about the business in the invitation or you have merged the Invitation with the Presentation and will find **failure**. We all make mistakes but successful people learn from the mistakes and constantly improve.

'Perfect Practice That Makes Perfect.' When your invitation is not working get some help with reviewing and tweaking it. When it is working, leave it alone and just get proficient at doing it over an over again and teaching it to others. The first invitation the prospect hears is also the first training for that prospect as they are likely to do what you did, not what you say to do.

The 3 Way Call is one of the most powerful tools in MLM. It is the most effective, the least expensive yet unfortunately one of the least used. Not using 3 Way Calls in almost all recruiting is a huge mistake. It is important to do it right. A lot of the success of a 3 Way Call is setup and posturing.

First, never put your prospect on a 3 Way Call unless they have seen the presentation. Doing so just makes it a two on one sales scenario and results in failure.

Make sure you have notified your intended expert or upline of your intention to make follow up calls and use them for a 3 Way Call. Text is best for this. You should do it way in advance if possible but never forget that the Expert is busy too, so text again right before the call. Make sure you get a positive agreement to do the call from the expert before proceeding. If you don't, you may find yourself very embarrassed as you get your prospect on the phone and can't get the expert.

When calling your prospect you must ask if they indeed have seen the presentation, unless you saw it with them, and what they saw that they liked the best. I recommend that question two or three times to find what they liked about your opportunity, as it will let you know what is important to them. Always remember, asking a positive question brings positive results. Don't ask negative questions. If they do, immediately show respect for their question and turn to the 3-way call.

Do not ask permission of your prospect. When they begin to ask questions just say: "I knew you would have questions and I want to get them answered for you. Please hold on a minute." Put them on hold and then dial your expert.

Once the expert answers let him know it is show time and who the prospect is. Then, switch over combining the three lines so all of you are in a conference conversation. Let the prospect know that you were lucky to catch your expert/mentor, as he or she is a very busy successful person.

> *You don't want a job; you want a business.*

Edify your expert to the prospect and edify your prospect to the expert. Your expert will then take over the call and edify you. You must remain silent unless called on by the expert.

Let the expert answer the questions and close or trail close the prospect. If you interrupt the expert while the call is going on, you are taking credibility away from your expert. Just let them speak.

At the end of the call the expert will either close the prospect and direct you to get them registered as a representative or direct you to take or send them to a local presentation. The expert will not tell the prospect what to do, but will instruct you and then welcome the prospect to the team and offer his personal assistance the same way they have just seen done.

Follow up is the key to success. If you are doing the business right, you are doing lots of invitations. You must keep good records and continue to politely follow up with your prospects. They will appreciate the politeness and persistence along with your good business practice of obviously keeping track of what has been said or done before.

As this book is a sequel to "Of Course You Can", by Steven List & Steve Thompson, I highly recommend you get a copy of that book to follow as your guide to getting started in MLM. It contains much of the how to as well as some very effective training programs that will get you to initial success.

17

Leads and Marketing Systems

*O*k, this won't make me popular with those out selling "Easy Way to Recruit" lead systems but, the only one they really work for are the lead sales people. You can generate more leads than you can ever use just by getting to know people and asking for referrals. If you know 50 and they each know 50 it is endless. And, I guarantee you know more than that.

Stick to working your warm market, people you already know and building your warm market by meeting new people and referrals. Never try to sell or pitch to strangers unless you need a good lesson in rejection. Instead, when you meet people concentrate on building relationships, friendships.

Talk to people you meet using **F.O.R.M**:

Family   **Their family and friends**

Occupation **Their Occupation**

Recreation **What they do for fun**

Money   **Do they have enough for things they love?**

When you talk about F.O.R.M. and take good notes you will not only learn about the person and build a relationship, you will gain the knowledge of how your product and business can improve their life.

You should not only resist the temptation to pitch new acquaintances but avoid the subject all together for the first three or four weeks you know someone. If they bring it up, answer their question briefly and then change the subject back to FORM. (i.e.: I am a professional networker with "XYZ" Company but tell me more about your kids.)

Always remember, asking positive questions brings positive results.

It only takes a moment for someone to feel it if your goal is only to sell your product or opportunity. There is plenty of time and after they know you, have corresponded or spoken to you a few times, they will be more genuinely curious about your business. They will want it more if they ask about it rather than you try to give it to them.

Relationship Marketing is all about the relationship so always keep that on your mind and in your daily practice. Ninety-five percent of the world does not like to sell and many don't like the ones that do. Be a friend sharing, rather than a salesman pushing.

Combine this with what we learned earlier and you will never run out of warm market. As a part time networker, or one that has a large team, it is important to not go for more than you can properly follow up with. I recommend contacting two prospects a day. Again, not at random, but from your prepared, written and prioritized list. Do this at least five days a week, keep good contact records and follow up. Along with that simply remember that this is Relationship Marketing. Invest some time every day in making new relationships. Make it a point to meet three new people every day. Don't try to sell them, try to make friends. Stay in touch with them and build the relationship over at least 21 days and they will be part of your warm market list and you will never run out of personal prospects.

How long does that take? Just a few minutes each day, Maybe five days a week. Besides building a magnificent prospect list you will gain the Networking Skills of listening, probing, caring and contact record keeping along with broadening your exposure and increasing your center of influence. It is often said that the best prospects are those that possess ERIC:

Entrepreneurship- **Entrepreneurial Skills and Past**

Resources- **Financial ability to start your business as well as the ability to make a large list of prospects.**

Influence- **Are they influential? Do people listen to and follow them?**

Consistency- **Do they have history of being consistent and seeing a job through?**

If that is true then shouldn't you become more like that every day? Become who you want to be friends with and recruit, and you will do so.

18

Developing Attitude and Team Culture

*W*e have all heard: "If you think you can or if you think you can't, you are probably right. You may not be able to control the circumstances around you but you can control how you react to them. To be a great leader you must look for the positive in things. You have to look for the opportunity hidden by the problem or just focus on getting around the problem. You must continually develop a get it done, winning attitude.

Everyone likes to be on a winning team. Accordingly, almost everyone looks to follow a leader with a winning attitude. You must be that leader and by doing that help others to do the same. I hate the calls or emails that start with "We have a huge problem". That tells me the person calling or writing is leaning toward negativity. It is time to try to gently remind the caller of the positive.

While I don't continue to work with repeatedly negative people, I do try to offer some positive thoughts. Perhaps it will rub off on them. At the very least it will make me feel better about myself as I walk away. **We are in the people helping people business.** Don't miss an opportunity.

Team culture is about winning attitude, respect for leaders, sharing openly and rejoicing in the success of others. It is about a positive winning attitude that permeates a large group of people that feel like a family, pulling together for financial freedom for all. There are simple rules that your mother probably tried to teach you.

> Anytime you are in question ask:
>
> 1st   What is best for the new person/people on the Team
>
> 2nd   What is best for the Team as a whole
>
> 3rd   What is best for you!
>
> Keep things in that order and most other things take care of themselves.

People like to belong and it is important to not only work together but arrange for social and recognition events as well. You know the saying: "People that play together, stay together". I like to host events and outings for my team. Not all of them, there are too many. But do it for the leaders and encourage them to do it for their leaders.

Always build for the next event. Not only will it increase productivity, but also it is the greatest of bonding times. Encourage everyone to go to the company events. Be proud of your team but do not make them stand out different from the other teams. Again, the whole company is One Team, not 'ours and theirs'. I like to use small tokens like Teamwork Lapel Pins. We can all see them without offending or putting off other teams within the company team.

Be assured. The members of your team that attend company events will be the true leaders. Others may talk a big story and add to the team but true leaders support company and team events. Take note of who comes. You will want to focus your efforts on helping them.

Everyone looks to follow a leader with a winning attitude.

As a new leader you should be hosting small events. Gatherings at the park or lake, dinners or other outings. Using your own home is a great way to go, as it makes it more personal. Don't do it all for everyone. Let everyone participate by bringing things and helping out. This is team building.

To this day, when I visit a new city to train and speak, I try to set up something social. It may be a luncheon for leaders, or frequently an early supper get together for the leaders in that area. Again, this is relationship marketing so it is important to continue to build relationships. The number of people that approach or write me to let me know they were touched by me being so "Normal and Approachable" continually rewards me. This is where I differ from many leaders.

There is an old culture in MLM that still dominates. It is based on people wanting to be in the inner circle. While I believe in building a special bond by meeting and spending special time with the top leaders, I do not want to be aloof, unapproachable or distant from the people that make my business successful. I am frequently early to presentations and trainings and spend that few minutes introducing myself to everyone possible. It is huge when you meet a new representative or prospect and then later when you are introduced they are positively surprised to have already met you personally.

One of the best things ever written about me was "Ordinary Man, Extraordinary Results". I go in the opposite direction of those that brag or list their accomplishments. If a talk is properly promoted and you are properly edified in the introduction, you need not talk about it. (Remember that when you are good you feel the need to talk about yourself but when you are great others talk about you.) **Start being great now!**

Get Excited!

Stay Focused!

Never Quit!

There is some creative liberty in public speaking and I use it to relax the audience and to have some fun. I often start by telling an audience that I was sent to speak to show that <u>anyone</u> can be successful. I tell them to listen for the next few minutes and it will become obvious. I like to ask things like: "How many of you were in the top half of your class in high school". I get a show of hands and then quickly add "it is people like me that make that possible". I tell them that the only thing that kept me out of Law School was college. I like to laugh at myself and get others to laugh with me. These are your new friends, act like it!

I have done that so many times that sometimes the introducer, having heard me before, will describe me as such and introduce me like he or she was introducing a good friend at a party. I am from the south (Texas) and rather than defend my southern dialect, I make fun of it and use stories to disarm pessimistic people and make sure the event is fun. (Keep in mind how many blue People are in the audience). Most of the best public speakers realize that it should not be a speech delivered, but rather a conversation with a large group of new friends.

Part of your attitude and culture must be to have fun. Most people are overworked, tired and unhappy with their traditional job or business and our industry should stay away from that with independence, enjoyment and self-fulfilling work of helping others with the joys of personal relationships. You can not only personally succeed but do so by focusing on the desires of others and take pleasure in truly making a difference in many lives. When done with the right attitude and culture, it is the perfect business.

19

Staying in Touch With Your Team

You should be very connected with your Team. Between emails, newsletters, text, conference calls, phone calls and live meetings/trainings; you can stay connected to hundreds, even thousands.

Stay Part Time. Yes, avoid quitting your job to early. In most cases, you should more than double your current income before you give up your regular job. Sometimes you just hate what you do so much that you leave early but **do not think** that by leaving your job you will grow faster in MLM. It is hard to recruit when you are desperate.

__Anyone__ can be successful.

Take a note from the great Jim Rohm. Jim says that you have a much easier time recruiting when you can say: "I have this part time business in the xyz business that pays me significant income. Would you like to see it?. It is psychology. If you are full time and make even 10 or 20 thousand it is not near as impressive as a part time person earning half that. Everyone is interested in something that takes less time and pays significant money.

This business is as much social as it is work. A modern MLM business runs on electronic media. While you don't want to overload people with email and text, it is important to send messages with some regularity. Sending messages once or twice a week with a positive message of current events or schedules and stories of success can do a lot for helping people feel in touch as a part of a team.

Email may be becoming a less effective form of communication in our business. Our instant gratification society has moved more and more to texting. The group forms of text include using Group Text Software and agents such as Twitter. I use group text to communicate with top leaders and get quick action. Many large leaders go to the extent of setting up geographical groupings of representatives enabling them to quickly get the word out to a specific territory. Most company systems will allow you to email specific territories and in the near future that may move to text as well.

Webinars are quickly taking the place formerly held by conference calls although conference calls are still the most simple and require no special equipment and work well even while on the move. We know that many people learn best from audio, more from visual and to a lesser extent from reading --although here you and I are. Webinars allow you to combine all of these information delivery systems for the broadest and most effective coverage.

While text may lack the personality touches of a phone call and personal conversation, it more than makes up for the deficiency with speed. Start using it early in your career because when you are blessed with a large team, you do not have the time for that many conversations. Texting is quick and usually a very clear form of communication. Be sure to sign your text and give your location, as you may not yet be stored in the receivers' phone and he or she will not know who or where you are.

I get multiple messages daily that go unanswered because I have no idea who it is or where it is from so my priority leans toward the ones I know. When you have a team of thousands you can't store them all in your phone. Properly worded texts with clear identification of the sender and the question or need usually gets an almost instant response. On the other hand, many just text and say I want to talk with you or please call and you have no way of knowing if you have the time. The caller may be asking things not in your control or interest or even be unrelated to your business.

To sum it up, if you are not into email, text, conference calls and webinars, you may be left behind. You must check email and text frequently and if you are not using Facebook, Linked-In and Twitter, you are behind the times. Electronic communication is your friend and can keep you in touch with thousands of people.

20

Working With Other Leaders

*Y*our business and your company will rise or fall on leadership. It takes many leaders to build a great company. You may not relate to them all but they are all important to your company's Success and thus yours. It is of utmost importance that you honor other leaders and welcome their groups to your events. Old school times kept people segregated by downline and that retarded the growth. Leaders should work together and offer help to each other and each other's teams. However, if you are asked for help by a rep from another team it is important to edify their leader and remind them that anything you say that differs from what their leader teaches should be left alone. Remind them that day-by-day they will rely on their own upline leadership so it is important that they stay in tune with that person.

In large group presentations there should never be Teams. We are all one Team in Public Presentations and should speak and act inclusive, not exclusive. A guest should never even be able to tell who is on what Team as you are all on the Company Team. You will find that if you give to other leaders and share your best rather than selfishly protect it, you will have much more Success in Relationship Marketing.

Leaders should also seek to build unified systems within the same company. When they don't it turns into theirs and ours and that has destroyed companies. No one leader or even group of leaders is always the holder of All Successful Ideas.

Try to always keep with the acronym, TEAM. Together, Everyone Achieves More!

When a prospect or new consultant comes into your business they may not understand Rank Titles. However, they will associate those titles with not only success but with closer representation of the company. The higher your title, the more people will think you are like an officer of the company. We know you are not, but you cannot know what you do not know and new people just don't know.

Try to always keep with the acronym, TEAM. Together, Everyone Achieves More!

With leadership should come the satisfaction of responsibility? Strive to take more responsibility and you will gain in leadership and that will help you achieve Rank Title. Once you understand that, Rank Title will step down a little in how you view leaders. Some have title and are lacking in leadership skills while others exhibit great leadership skills but have not yet achieved Rank Title. However, we should always treat Rank Title holders with respect.

When working with other leaders, on your team or not, remember a company's success will rise and fall with leadership. You have the responsibility to be inclusive, not exclusive. Each interaction with others are chances to not only improve your leadership skill but to help the other to improve as well. Helping other leaders, even those not on your team will greatly improve your business. This business is very different from traditional businesses and that is one of our greatest advantages.

You should not hold down others or try to do better than them to reach the top. Quite the opposite is true. You must help and lift up other leaders as you all go to the very top...together!

What a blessing our industry is when leaders work together, lift one another up and rise to the top.

21

Choosing the Right Opportunity & Seeing the Job Through

*W*hile I have seen some people prosper in a very short time, for most of us it takes time. I have been in the industry for over 18 years and while I had some good Success over the years, it was sticking around that made me a Top Earner.

I first started in the Vitamin Business with Herbalife. It is a great company and it was that experience that opened my eyes to the opportunity for personal growth and financial growth in Network Marketing. I made some money but found I was not passionate enough about the products to deal with them every day. I kept looking at different opportunities but it was years before I joined another.

My second one was Excel Communications. It was a great company and revolutionary in combining a service, Long Distance Telephone Service with Relationship Marketing. What a great combination, as they truly saved people money on a service they almost always had to have. But, my timing was off and I learned a valuable lesson.

The company did over a billion in sales the year I joined and had already expanded into all 50 states. Long distance was a doomed product as cell phones and broadband services took over and the company was slow to innovate. After about eight years there, they were gone and I had only my experience to show for it. Many left the industry and I was dismayed for a bit but resolved to never quit!

A couple of years later I was invited to a new company in the Skin Care Business. They got me when they said they wanted me for my expertise. No one had ever said that before ☺. But I did not look closely at the financial strength and management.

To be a great leader you must look for the positive in things.

Management had hardly any MLM Experience and although they were backed by a Billionaire, he really had not committed enough to get them off the ground. After just a few months they were cutting commissions, restricting growth and trying to market extremely overpriced products. That was a recipe for disaster and I was thankful just to give up my position. I moved to the Travel Network Marketing Industry.

The new company I chose was not that well financed but their product did not require much. They could and did open the whole USA right away without much investment. They went on to open many countries. They were some of the best network Marketers I ever worked with but the product was just not very profitable. Their focus was so heavy on selling the business that they were always in question.

I got in early and had the skills so it was my first time to be a Top 20 Money Earner. I made it to #12 but realized that most could never make much with it and the company itself would always be competing for the MLM Dollar. I left and they have done well. However, not the kind of well I was looking for!

About that time I got a call about Ambit Energy. I was very familiar with the concept from my years in Excel. Ambit Energy had what I was looking for.

The financial backing was from some huge names in Financial

Success. They were not borrowing money to fund the start up and had already hired incredibly Successful Management before they even had customers. Not only was it early in their business but also it would continue to be early for the next 10 or 15 years, as it would take that long to expand. And it was the largest deregulation in Free World History. That is what I needed to see, and I got started.

Now I would not recommend that start up time to most people. They did not have the systems in place nor much market open. There were virtually no meetings, no video and only the beginnings of web support. But they had the plan, the money and the commitment and I knew I had the skill. Newer people in the industry will be way better off joining now, after the formulation stage yet still ahead of the bulk of the expansion and momentum.

Now here is the part many do not want to hear. I became a Top Money Earner not just in my company but also in the industry as a whole from hard work. **This is Network Marketing. Not Net-Wish-Marketing or Net-Luck-Marketing, it is Work!** I worked harder for the last few years than ever before. I traveled more, struggled more and face more problems, setbacks and rejections. However, I now live a life that most dare not dream of. I am writing this chapter on my Luxury Yacht in route from southern Florida to New England for the summer. I live on my Dream Game Ranch and fly to presentations on my private plane. My future is secure and I have Financial Freedom because of my work in the Network Marketing Industry. Many still say: "It Won't Work". Many thousands of other MLM pros along with myself know that what they really mean is that "They Won't Work".

I was fortunate to find the Insurance industry and Residual Income in my early 20s. Learning about Residual Income led me to a certain level of Financial Freedom and a good life. However, when you combine the extreme leverage of MLM with true Residual Income from a service that almost everyone uses and combine that with a business model that rewards you for helping others, you have the ingredients to make your dreams come true!

I wish you the best in your business. Believe in yourself, your company and your future.

22

Expecting Success!

*D*o you have lofty goals? Have you spent some time setting those goals and do you know what it takes to achieve them? Freedom is not free. Are you willing to pay the price for Financial Freedom? These are just a few of the questions you must answer before you can set the route for success.

As I said before, I was willing to put in a huge burst of energy and very hard work for a few years so that I could have the life I now enjoy. It is important to realize that most multi-millionaires from athletes and movie stars to many business owners and CEOs do not have the kind of income we are talking about here.

Now that I enjoy my own airplanes, a luxury yacht, a dream ranch, beautiful homes and a multi-million dollar residual income, I want you to achieve this and more. I want to help you achieve all of your dreams. However, you must realize how much work goes in to getting where I am. So if you prefer to only work only ¼ or ½ as hard and still make very significant income, you still must be clear that there is no free ride to success.

There is a wonderful life ahead if you are willing to put in the hard work and dedicate yourself to helping others. You can live your dreams. The next few years will go by very quickly. I am so glad that I paid the price for a brief time and now live the results for a lifetime.

Most people come into the Network Marketing Industry with dreams of easy money and quick if not instant success. Others come in with just the hope of a little extra money to help them get through life. The former is a wish or maybe a dream but definitely not a goal or a plan. The latter is the backbone of the industry but you will usually only achieve what you set your sights on.

For years, MLM was just that to me. For years I saw it as a way to generate some extra income that I could use to invest and improve my life. It worked. For years I made only a few thousand dollars but was fortunate to invest it well and it did improve my life. I did not really believe I could achieve huge financial success. My belief held me back and I still found success.

A few years ago I realized that not only was this industry my calling but that I had the skills and desire and this could be truly life changing. I quit using my "spare" time for Real Estate, Active Investing & Trading as well as dropping my Music Management Company and begin to focus all of my time (Other than my core Insurance Business) on reaching for the stars in Networking. I realized that although I saw myself as an extreme multi-task person, I was really not committed to becoming a professional networker.

There I was at a point of change in my life. I embraced my career along with the fear and hard work required and began to hold myself out as a professional in Network Marketing. I began to announce it with pride. I quit hiding behind my other business interests to protect my ego from the possible failure to go all the way in MLM.

It set me free. As I cut off retreating down other paths it cleared the way to the top. There is a wonderful view from the top. If you want to climb to the top of this mountain, you're going to have to step off the boat and become laser focused on MLM Success.

I had been a student for a decade but now I began to truly step into the role. It was time to embrace leadership, pay the price, do the time, suffer the failures and not only embrace but demand success from myself. It became a quest of liberation from being and living a normal life.

If you are willing to put in the hard work and dedicate yourself to helping others. You can live your dreams.

The last few years (8 of my 19 years in MLM) have been some of the toughest and most rewarding of my life. I've traveled more, missed out on more home activities, got stood up more, and faced more trials and challenges than ever before. I've also experienced more joy, learned more, met more new friends, learned more new cultures, become a better leader and reached Financial Freedom.

When I joined my current company they were a start up. They only had 13 employees and a few hundred consultants/representatives. We all pulled together to develop systems. At that time, there were not many tools. No videos, only one website, a work in progress PowerPoint Presentation and only a couple of ongoing Group Presentations.

It was a humble and tough beginning but offered a huge opportunity to experienced people that could and would see the job through. I did not wait for tools or systems to be developed for us. We developed the systems or just worked harder with what we had. Many a presentation or training was done on a white board or a sheet of paper.

As it was a Dallas based company, there were a couple of meetings around Dallas. I lived in Austin, Texas and although we started a presentation in the Suburbs of Austin, the city itself was not deregulated. I had thousands of friends and clients in Austin and

San Antonio but to this day those are areas where we can't sell energy. I knew I had to travel to make it happen.

I began to drive all over Texas. I went to Houston for several days every week. Each day I would get in the car with a new prospect or consultant and drive around having them introduce me to their friends and prospects. I did not wait for them; I did the invitation for them. Usually I did that with more than one person a day inviting people to the presentation that night. I set up the presentation with help from new folks and then I usually did the entire presentation. It was hard work and made for really long days but yes, my business began to succeed.

I set a lofty goal of building a team of at least 2500 consultants my first year and set my schedule to get that done. Our Houston Team grew and expanded to South Texas, West Texas, and East Texas, back into Dallas and along the Gulf Coast. At 3 months it looked doubtful for me reaching my goals but I just wanted the rewards so much that I just worked harder, went more places and talked to more people. I spoke to anyone that would talk to me.

At the 6-month mark it looked like I had a shot but it was still a long way to 2500. At 9 months it was rolling and geometric progression had carried me beyond the goal. By the time I finished my first year and we were about to expand out of Texas for the first time and there were over 5000 on our team. The company announced New York City!

I had only been to NYC once before and that was on a leisure trip with the Travel Company. However, I knew it would be the key to market share for the future as NYC is the Economic Capital of the World and NYC is connected to the world!

I simply did what worked. The same hard work that paid off in Texas would pay off in NYC. Unfortunately, I only knew about three people in NYC and two said no. But I asked everyone I knew anywhere: "Whom do you know that knows anyone in NYC". It worked and I soon had people to work with. I felt my dreams were about to come true.

I spent every other week for 6 months in NYC. Each day was the same, with early mornings leading to long days of riding with people to meet people to invite to the presentations that night. Again I brought the equipment, set up the meeting, did the presentation and the training and stayed to answer the last question. For a long time I had my dinner at about 10:30 at night with a few excited new consultants before returning to my modest hotel room to rest for the next day. Each night I had the satisfaction of knowing I was doing what it takes!

Do today what others won't, and have tomorrow what others don't!

On my week off of NYC I visited every market in Texas. We had some good up and coming leaders but it was still important that I was there to help them. There was no need for time off. My passion was strong and my dreams were coming into view. Soon, we opened Illinois in the Northern Chicago Suburbs and I was off to a new place to repeat the same process.

By then, NYC had some good leaders developing and I moved to every 3rd week in NYC with a week in Texas and a week in Chicago. Nothing was different, as I was still one of the few that would pay the price to work in the new areas and the old saying came true.

Chicago took an unexpected downturn, as our license to operate did not come through as expected. We went months without being able to get customers and thus get paid. Many if not most in that area just gave up. I knew that the flip side of challenge was opportunity. Thanks to a few strong folks on my team, we kept it going just at a slower pace. I focused more of my attention on the newly opened Upstate NY. It was becoming easier as our history of success made things a bit smoother but you still had to do the work.

We expanded to seven other states since then. I knew that none would be without difficulty and setbacks, and grew in experience as I traveled to every new territory. Usually I was the one setting up the first meetings and leading the charge. What a blessing! I reveled in the chance to have a personal impact on so many lives. Not until the recent opening of California did I step back and not be the first one doing the meetings. Of course by then, I was blessed with a great number of leaders and a team of over 80,000. The MLM Machine was working.

There were a lot of days that it was tough out there. There were a lot of lonely times with not much to rely on but your own resilience and it made me a much stronger person. I truly learned to focus on what others were going through. There was not time to focus on problems, just solutions. I had become a problem solver not a problem finder. When you ran into barriers you just went around, through them or took another route. But, you did not stop!

It was a very simple beginning: Just work hard and go way out of your way to help other people. Stay focused on the goal and constant leadership development. Never let anyone steal your dreams by turning your focus to what won't work. **Lead from the front and others will follow.**

The whole theory of MLM is that you can compact 40 years of

working into just 10 years or less. Because of the timing right now, you can cut that in half. If you are willing to do more, help more, give of yourself and your time more and work like never before, you too could find yourself living your dreams. I am not saying you will earn a fortune, only that you could!

This book is dedicated to that cause. I wish you the best as you decide to step up your level of dedication and if you do, I will see you at the Top!

Get Excited!   Stay Focused!   Never Quit!

23

Training & Blogs

Believe in Yourself

(Training Notes)

1) Believe in Yourself, Your Company, Leaders & Executives

2) Give Yourself Permission!

3) Take responsibility for your own success

4) Be open for business

5) Work with a schedule

6) Set long and short-term goals with self-rewards

7) Look for ways to serve

8) Learn to follow to learn to lead

9) Don't spend too much time with the wrong people

10) Plant the Flag!

     a. Take massive action!

     b. Don't let the Dream Stealers Win!

     c. Don't put down or lift up the competition

11) Be a sorter, not a seller!!!!

12) Prepare yourself for Success

13) Reprogram yourself with declarations

14) Read and Listen. Always be a student

15) Think like a Wealthy Person

16) See the job through

      a.   Focus

      b.   Excitement

      c.   Commitment

"Accountability Teams"

A Commitment to Success

All successful business people have a system! Success in our business requires that the system be simple, duplicable, pragmatic and consistent. The Team provides the most successful method of business presentation to a prospect. This system is to put large numbers of people in front of the Team Business Presentation, on a consistent basis!

☐ Prepare a written list of prospects. Do not limit or edit your list or you will limit your success. Our task is to offer the opportunity to everyone, and help them make their own decision!

☐ Write one prospect's name, telephone number, and other pertinent information at the top of an index card (i.e.: name, number, address, occupation, reasons they need opportunity, and etc.)

☐ File all index cards in alphabetical section, (stored for prioritizing).

☐ Using the prioritization system of your choice, place two cards, from alpha section in each of the calendar day sections. (Use more than two if you want to contact more than the minimum.)

☐ Each day, contact the two prospects in today's section. Try to set an appointment to take the prospect to a Team Business Presentation or Video.

☐ If the prospect says yes, make note of the conversation and place it in the appropriate date slot so you can reconfirm the appointment on that day.

☐ If the prospect says no (not now), ask if you can check back next week, or in a few weeks (or months). Make a note of your conversation, on the card, and file it in the appropriate daily or monthly slot.

☐ Each day, send an email message to your 2 or 3 teammates (utilizing a distribution list), reporting on the results of your contacts and the names of who you are to contact tomorrow.

☐ Weekly, have a conference call with your teammates, (utilizing three way calling), and discuss the week's results (i.e.: appointments made, new distributors, objections and etc.)

It is very important that you keep your system up to date and that you make your contacts. If you have a schedule conflict, be sure to make up those contacts you miss so that no one misses out on the opportunity.

Building Leadership Builds Success

(Training Notes)

- Primary Goal – Make significant income, build leadership and promote to High Rank with high income.

- Single Most Important Ingredient to Successfully Lead is to lead from the front

- Never quit working with a winner because of coding.

- Personal development. Consistently read, listen and learn

- Work with the right people

- Recognize Quitters (But maybe they are not really quitters)

- 72 Hour Rule (This goes throughout career)

- Recruit up, but do not neglect people.

- Build fast to save Consultant and find worker.

- Drill down for success. Work the bottom.

- Work with people that deserve your time

- Group Time VS Personal Time

  o MCs & RCs use same ratio – 90/10

  o SC Ratio – 60/40

  o EC Ratio – 40/60

  o Who gets the time?

  o How do you allocate your time?

o 3 Personal Rule

- Stacking

- Pitfalls of Welfare Atmosphere

- Creating Dependence rather than Independence

- Huge Loss of Residual Income

- When to stack

- Friends & Family

  o Same out of town location with probable working relationship

  o To get SC # 5

- Building RCs and SCs

o Building RCs is the #1 way to build Success!

o #1 Place to quit = RC. #2 Place to quit = SC.

o Identify runners/leaders & Build RCs

o RCs – 72 Hour Rule

o Why are there 3 or 4 SCs in same leg?

o Work deep – Disregard Levels

o Identify Individuals – Build in Teams

- o Allocate Percentages by Teams

- o Create MO/Atmosphere of Success

- Income Goals

  - o Setting Strong but Realistic Expectations

  - o MC/RC/SC/EC/NC

- Tools for Success

  - o **Ambit University**

  - o **www.NeverQuitSteve.com**

  - o **www.AmbitPros.com**

Get Excited - Stay Focused - Never Quit!

Power Pitch Recruiting System

Welcome to the "Power Pitch Audio/Video Recruiting System",

This system will help you build momentum using an Automated System.

One of the most frequent downfalls in building a large Network Marketing Team is caused by loss of discipline due to excitement. Yes, that's true. We all know we must use a simple, effective and duplicable system that removes the need for highly developed skills and sales ability. We know that if those on our Team do not easily copy it, it will hinder rather than enhance our growth. However, we frequently just can't resist putting ourselves more heavily into the process by personal presentation and long conversations and even debates about our business. Never fear, there is a cure.

We have a simple and substantially complete, multiple step process that works like a flow chart system filling the funnel of success. If followed, the results are substantial and easily measurable, not only in your personal results, but also in the duplication and even multiplication that results in Momentum! We urge you to follow it like the instructions for baking a cake or re-building an engine. Skip a few steps and you may seem to be taking a shortcut to success, but end up on a side path that leads to a fallen cake or useless and poor operating engine. Success is found by sticking to a system and following the path to Success.

We wish you the best as you learn to use a system that works real hard, so you don't have to.

Tools required for using this system:

- Computer, Internet Access and Reliable Internet Service

- Power Pitch Voice Mail System

- Websites. (Already there if active Consultant/Representative)

- Energy Gold Rush or equivalent capture page with optional auto-responder.

- Flyers/Bookmarks/Sizzle Cards/Business Cards etc.

- Time period required for Successful Test and implementation of system: 60 – 90 days

First let's talk about the tools:

There are many sources for a voicemail system. Make sure to choose an inexpensive one that has the option to send you text of email when you have a message.

Company Website

Capture/Landing Page: You may use any, but the easiest and least expensive is **www.EnergyGoldRush.com/(YourNickname)**.

Flyers/Bookmarks/Sizzle Cards/Business Cards etc. Get the word out. Be creative on style, but don't change the wording. Too much information will ruin the success.

60 – 90 Days. Success does not happen overnight, but it can happen very quickly. Use it yourself so you become proficient. Give the system enough time to work and it may change your life. The people brought in using the system will be very likely to succeed, as they tend to build their business using the same system that brought them into the business.

Setting up your system:

1. Make sure your Company Websites are operating and you have updated your payment information so it does not go down causing your system to stop.
2. Obtain a Voice Messaging System to carry your Power Pitch Number.

   Sizzle Line Download

   Steve Thompson's MP3 Sizzle Recording

   (Others to follow)
3. Order Sizzle Cards/Bookmarks/Flyers from vender using your design and using the suggested wording.
4. Go to **www.EnergyGoldrush.com** and register your own site. All of the needed information and instruction is available from that website, as well as training on its use. (Optional: Add the iContact system as offered through Energy Gold Rush and learn to use its functions.)

Working the system:

Step One: The Audio Sizzle Message

1. The purpose of this system is to facilitate exposing a large number of people to the Opportunity with minimum personal explanation and presentation. This is the very basis of the system! Trust in the system and do not add or subtract from it as you may limit your success. Please resist the temptation to add your own conversations, presentations, and explanations. Do not derail the system by allowing the prospect to control the conversation, and thus the system, by asking the questions and getting you to

answer them. (The person asking the questions controls the conversation). Let the system work!

Start conversations with an excitement statement about what you have found.

"I Found Something Great That May Change Our Financial Life Forever!"

Then ask these Four Questions:

1. What do you know about Energy Deregulation?
2. How many people do you know that use Electricity or Natural Gas?
3. Would they like to pay less or even potentially get their energy for free?
4. If I can guide you through a brief system, would you give me a few minutes to learn about a company that will pay you significant income to help others save on their home utilities?
   It only takes a few minutes and starts with listening to a 3 Minute Recorded Message. There is no obligation.

Hand them a flyer/sizzle card/bookmark with only the words:

Change Your Financial Life!

Earn Significant Income Helping Others Save Money on Their Home Utilities

3 Minute Recorded Message

(XXX) XXX-XXXX

You may add graphics and use different colors to enhance, but DO NOT ADD MORE WORDS!

Ask the prospect to please call the number on the card and listen to the overview. If they want more information, just leave their name and number at the end of the 3-minute recording. They may ask for more information right now, but it is critical that you avoid that by saying, "Please just listen to the message. We have a system that works hard so we don't have to. You will enjoy it!"

Remember, the goal of this message is to be a filter. As a filter, it is not designed to "Hook" the wrong people but rather to eliminate the large number of people that just aren't interested. That way you only talk again to those that are interested. It is widely known that many fail in this business by spending too much time talking to the wrong people. **Success comes from getting the message to a large number of prospects.** Let the system work for you!

2. Check your Voicemail at least daily. As people leave messages you will receive an email that you have Messages. Go to your voicemail back office (Click the link in the message) or call and check the messages by phone. The more Sizzle Cards you give out, the more messages you will receive. And these are prospects that WANT TO TALK TO YOU!

At each step of this process be alert to prospects that are extremely excited and are ready to get started. As we feel there is no comparison to a Large, Exciting Group Business Presentation, you should always invite a prospect to the Group Presentation. If they are ready, go directly to that step. If not, go to the next step in the process. (And at anytime someone is ready to get started, quit talking and Register them as a Consultant!!!)

Step Two: The Video Message

Assuming the person left a message, you should call them right away. The more you delay, the more time you leave for them to stray from the path. Never let a call back go more than 24 hours from when they left the message. If you are getting more response than you can handle, teach the system to your down line and spread the leads.

The Call Back:

1. Thank the person for completing step one by listening to the 3-minute audio message. Let them know that it is your job to supply them with additional information. However first you need to ask a few questions to see: "if they could

possibly be a match for us". These are very simple questions and must stay just this brief. Write the answers down to start learning about your prospect and developing a relationship.

Ask:

First, let me verify your contact information. Please confirm your name, phone number and email address.

We are expanding in many areas. Where do you live?

What kind of work do you do now, or did in the past that might make you a candidate for our Team?

Can you devote 5 to 7 hours a week to a business of your own so that you develop a significant income?

Then let them know you appreciate them working through the system and that it shows their ability to work with our Success System.

Ask:

Do you have something to write with as I am going to give you a website to visit to complete step two of the process?

*Please visit **www.EnergyGoldRush.com/(YourNickname)**. You will watch a brief video presentation that will explain our business. If it makes sense to you, we will then arrange for you to get all of your questions answered so that you* *can make a decision to join our Team. As always, there is no obligation and we appreciate you working with us.*

You will be asked to register to view the video and that information only goes back to us, and we already have it. It merely verifies for us that you have completed Step Two. I will also email you a link to the site; so if you need any assistance, don't hesitate to reply to my message.

Here is my personal phone number: (XXX) XXX-XXXX. Please give me a call once you have watched the video. (Very few call back. But if they do they are very hot prospects. You must make the follow up calls!)

Thanks, and we look forward to visiting with you.

You must resist the urge to tell them more or answer more questions. Don't be rude, just let them know that our system is quite complete and we appreciate their patience so that the system can work for them.

Now comes the fun part! When they log into Gold Rush, you will get an email letting you know that they are watching the video. This is your alert that you have the hottest of prospects. A prospect that is informed and has the information from a reliable system is a pleasure to work with.

Now it's time to call again.

Say:

Thank you for completing step two. You have shown that you may very well be just the kind of person that we love to work with. I would like to invite you to a Live Corporate Overview so you can see all of this for yourself, as well as meeting many of the Top Leaders on our Team. Is Tuesday good for you or would Thursday Be Better? (Always give two options rather than ask a yes or no question.)

If they agree to come to the presentation, let them know how much you look forward to seeing them and introducing them to all of the fun people on the Team. Let them know you will either pick them up or re-confirm a couple of hours before the Overview. Then you should contact your upline or sideline and ask them to call the prospect to re-confirm and make them feel welcome.

The Upline would call and say:

"Hi _____. My business partner tells me you may be a great match with our Team and we are looking forward to meeting you on (Confirm the details of the Overview Time and Location). Thanks and we look forward to meeting you in person."

This not only makes them feel welcome, but also helps insure that they will be at the presentation.

If they hesitate on the Overview Presentation, it is time for a 3 Way Call. Let them know that you are about to put them on the phone with a very successful person that can answer all of their questions. Ask them to hold and do the 3 Way with you upline or cross line. Frequently this results in a new Consultant, but the goal is to just move them to the next step, which is the live presentation. If there is not a presentation, use the 3 Way Call and or the Monday Night Business Presentation Call.

At this point you move to Step Three and host them at a Live Business Presentation. Follow the system for Live Business Presentations and ask the closing questions at the end. Please go to **www.(YourTeamTrainingSite).com** and review that training as well.

Your success will come from introducing large numbers of people to this system and following the system as closely as possible. The moment you meet the prospect or they pick up a flyer, you are also training them to use the same system.

That is Duplication, which leads to Multiplication. And in turn, that leads to huge successful momentum!

This system is easily adaptable to advertising and flyer distribution. A brief discussion of that follows.

Flyers:

Think in hundreds and thousands. They should be bright and colorful. They must not be wordy or try to give too much information. The only goal of the Flyers/Book Marks/Sizzle Cards is to get people to listen to the message. If you give them more information, they may not.

The most critical words are: "3 Minute Recorded Message". That lets the prospect know that no one is going to answer the phone and try to sell anything to them. And that it only takes 3 minutes.

Do not put them on windshields etc. where it will just give you a bad name for being trashy. They are best when handed to people or placed on a counter with a sign that says "Please Take One". Ask for permission to place them at stores, dry cleaners, restaurants, convenience stores, service stations and etc. You will find that they are glad for you to put some on their counter. Don't do it without permission or they will cause more trouble that good.

One great method is to put a large one on bulletin boards with tear offs that just say "3 Minute Message – (XXX) XXX-XXXX", that way the flyer stays up for all to read and the individual takes the tear off.

Ads:

Ads can eat up your money in a hurry, so be careful. If you do advertise, the ads should be small and not contain any more information than the Flyers. If you use radio, you should repeat the phone number 3 times. Very short radio commercials or very brief ads in the right places may get you a lot of calls. Have fun with it.

But remember, this is Relationship Marketing. Nothing compares with calling people you know or meeting people in person and establishing a relationship. Allow it to grow and you will have much more success.

This system also works very well for a new consultant as they approach their friends.

First, they must complete the Success Passport (Available on **www.AmbitPros.com**). **DO NOT SHORTCUT YOUR SUCCESS BY NOT MAKING A LIST OF EVERYONE YOU KNOW.** After you help a new person create and prioritize their list, you just use this system as a way to introduce those prospects to Ambit. It is much better than just sending a new consultant out to talk about something they are new at doing!

Encourage them to give out the number to their prospects or give your new consultants a stack of cards. Encourage them to get their prospects to listen to the message and then follow the system all the way through.

Not knowing what to say or how to approach their friends holds a lot of people up. This system can solve that. If they use your number, they must tell their prospects to be sure and leave on the message that they are friend of the new consultant. Of course that means you get the messages and that enables you to make the calls with the new consultant.

Let the law of large numbers work for you. Follow the system and let the system do most of the work.

We suggest a 90-day concentrated blitz with this system. It takes a little preparation and a little practice to get the call back system down. Practice it with someone first. It is a simple system, so become an expert, and it will earn you a fortune.

If you find that the system is not working as well as you would like, review what you have been doing. Frequently, the system is suffering because you are **just saying too much!** It is time to go back to letting the system do the talking and keep your explanations/presentations out of the way.

Stick to the system and find Momentum!

Power Pitch Sample Script

Hello, and thanks for taking the time to make this call. Have the current economic times affected your income or how you feel about your future job security? Or perhaps in today's environment do you think that it'd simply be a good idea to have some other source of secure business income coming to you every month. Or, are you simply open to looking at new and exciting business opportunities that could allow you to dramatically change your lifestyle? If so, listen on.

My name is Steve Thompson. I am an Independent Consultant with a Cutting edge Energy Company that is a Licensed Public Utility, and have set out to sell and deliver Electricity at reduced rates. We are also in position to take advantage of the Energy Markets in many other states, as Energy Deregulation sweeps across America. Americans demand a choice, and deregulation will create the competition necessary to reduce the rates for all!

We are looking for sharp, ambitious people, from all backgrounds, technical and non-technical, sales and non-sales, who would like the opportunity to work flexible hours from home, as an independent contractor for our company and make a sizeable income, even on a very limited part time basis.

The pay plan that we have in place allows you to make excellent cash income on an immediate basis for your efforts, but more importantly, also allows you to earn ongoing product commission and profit sharing that come to you every month on a permanent, residual basis. We have the opportunity to receive income, every time people flip on a light switch, use their air conditioning or simply turn on the TV or Stereo!

Our Team is helping provide Electricity to Residential Users, at significant savings. This is a service that people use every day, and we need people at many different skill and career levels to join our Team and help us promote our company's services.

Whether you are a college student who wants to make a few extra hundred dollars a month, or busy professional who would like to build a solid income with a minimum investment of your time, you'll find that our company can provide what you are looking for.

If you are coach able, and can devote at least a few hours a week to a business enterprise, of your own, then we can teach you how to be successful as a member of our team.

So if you are serious about wanting to develop a part time, or full time income with a solid company, with a proven Management Team, then simply get back with the person that put you on this call, and they will provide you with more information at no obligation, about the opportunities available through our company.

The De-regulation of Energy will be the greatest redistribution of wealth in our lifetimes. 400 Billion dollars will move from a few big monopolies, to Entrepreneurial Companies and Individuals. It will only happen one time, and it is happening right now!

Not taking advantage of the income available to you in this huge economic shift could be a terrible financial mistake.

The Future is Bright! – The Opportunity is Electric!

With that, thanks for calling, and have a super day.

Cold Market Recruiting
By Steve Thompson & Ronnie Tanksley

We must remember that this is Relationship Marketing. We must put the relationship first. It is not wise to pitch strangers on your opportunity. Your goal is to consistently make new friends to add to your warm market list. Do not talk about the opportunity for at least 21 days, unless they aggressively try to find out about it.

Each time the subject of what you do for a living comes up you should resist and re-direct the conversation back to your new friend. You will find that everyone loves to talk about themselves and in doing so will tell you all the information you need. Once you have interacted with them as friends for a few weeks they will be much more open to your opportunity.

MEETING NEW PROSPECTS

- Local Cleaners
- Grocery Stores
- School Functions
- Restaurants
- DMV
- Coffee Shops
- Ball Games

ENGAGE IN FRIENDLY CONVERSATION

- Are you from around here?
- Do you have a family?
- Tell me about your family?

- How is the food here?
- Those are nice glasses.
- I like your shoes. Where did you get them?

MAKE A NEW ACQUAINTANCE

- F.O.R.M (Family, Occupation, Recreation, Money)
  Talk to people about F.O.R.M. and they will open up to you.
  It also supplies you with the information about the prospect
  that will determine why they need or want your opportunity.

**People will be more inclined to look at anything you ask of
them after you have built a relationship with them. Be
sincere!**

YOUR COLD MARKET LIST

- Contact New Prospects in 24 to 48 hours
- Always add new acquaintances

CONSULTANT'S FIRST MEETING WITH YOUR COLD MARKET PROSPECT

- 15 To 20 minute coffee meeting
- Focus on the prospect
- Let them talk about themselves

WHEN TO MENTION OPPORTUNITY – AFTER 21 DAYS

- Ask the prospect to look at the opportunity, after you have
  built a relationship.

- Or, you can ask the prospect if they know any motivated people interested in looking at an opportunity to make additional income.

HOW TO EXPOSE THE OPPORTUNITY

- Magazine
- Link to Website
- Live Corporate Overview
- One on One with Video

5-2-6 Blitz

Shawn Cornett & Damien Pechacek

526 Blitz Outline & Action Plan

(This outline provides a high level overview of the 526 Blitz system but we highly recommend you watch and take notes on the full video training that details the process at **www.AmbitPros.com/526-blitz** before starting your blitz)

526 Blitz Process Outline

Step 0 – Preparation

Prepare for your blitz by getting setup with EGR (EnergyGoldRush) & making a starter list of at least 50 prospects you can run through the following 526 blitz sorting process…

Step 1 - Invitation

Invite everyone on your list to review the 5 minute AmbitPros intro/sorting video on your EGR website. If after reviewing the video your prospect only expresses interest in being a customer, simply ask for another 5 minutes with their bill in hand so you can explain the process, value proposition and get them enrolled. If you've exposed at least 30 people to the sorting video you should end up with a bare minimum of five customers well within the 28 days needed for Jumpstart 1 and you should also have about 10 prospects that you can move to the next step…

Step 2 – Presentation

Immediately direct all prospects interested in the opportunity and/or free energy to review a full presentation, which can be a meeting if one is coming up soon or you can immediately direct them to the presentation page on EGR or any one of the other tools available like DVDs, magazines, webinars, etc. Out of the 10 or so prospects who review a full business presentation you will likely have about half of them move on to the next step…

Step 3 – Validation

After prospect has reviewed a full presentation, it's time to bring in some validation in the form of a 3 way call or you can bring them out to a meeting for another look and get the validation in person from a local leader. Out of the five or so that make it this far you will likely get about half who go on to enroll as consultants at which point it's time for…

Step 4 – Duplication

Immediately upon enrollment walk your new consultant through this same 526 Blitz action plan so you can help them enroll their first couple consultants at which point you promote to Regional Consultant!

Meeting Etiquette

REMEMBER: The focus is **always** on the guests. Everyone is to assume that this is the very first time a Guest has seen the Ambit Opportunity.

1. Roles at the meeting
    a. Introducer
        1) Keeps the Guest as the main focus
        2) gets the crowd's attention
        3) silences mobile phones
        4) briefly tells their background and their "why"
        5) introduces the First Speaker
    b. First Speaker
        1) Keeps the Guest as the main focus
        2) thanks the Introducer
        3) briefly tells their background and their "why"
        4) presents the company, industry and service
        5) introduces the Second Speaker
    c. Second Speaker
        1) Keeps the Guest as the main focus
        2) thanks the First Speaker
        3) briefly tells their background and their "why"
        4) presents the compensation plan
        5) introduces the Closer or special guest
    d. Closer
        1) Keeps the Guest as the main focus
        2) thanks all of the Speakers
        3) briefly tells their background and their "why"
        4) presents the 5 points (from the script)

      5) Asks the guests to join and circle up for questions.
- e. Consultant attending meeting
  - 1) Keeps the Guest as the main focus (whether they have one or not)
  - 2) Ensures guests have seats.
  - 3) Edifies speakers and presenters
  - 4) Watches time and does not linger too long in back socializing
  - 5) Contributes to meeting (applauds, laughs, etc. when appropriate)
  - 6) Does not bring negatives to the meeting.
- f. Guest
  - 1) Watch, listen, ask questions.
- g. Greeter
  - 1) Welcome guests at door
  - 2) Direct them to the sign in table
- h. Sign-in Table Greeter
  - 1) Sign in folks on correct form (use multiple forms, it's crowded)
  - 2) Direct folks to take a seat quickly

Other notes:

- Consultants should edify other consultants that have guests. Do not intrude on other consultant's guests (unless asked to by the inviting consultant).
- Consultants should not talk strategies or talk to their upline about problems at the business presentation. That should be for a private meeting, not around guests or other new Consultants.

Samples of Blogs Sent to Team

One of the Most Important Messages I Ever Wrote

We are fortunate to be in Ambit, right now! Not only was the NYC Leadership Launch fantastic, but also I was fortunate to spend a little time with our Executives and they are full of good news and huge forecasts. Here is what is going on.

Jere let us know that even though we are debt free and profitable, Ambit raised millions more in capital, just to be ready to take advantage of the timing in our marketplace. ALL of Ambit's systems were redone in 2009 and Ambit is ready for the largest growth year ever. He called it 2010, the WOW Year. I want to be part of that. Be sure to get to the Leadership Launch coming to your area so you can hear all of the information, directly from our CEO, Jere Thompson, Jr.

Chris went over some of the real numbers. We were number 46 on the list of largest MLMs by dollar amount last year. That was based on 2008 sales, so prepare yourself for Ambit to move way up the charts as our 2009 sales were almost double. And, 2010 looks like it will dwarf that!

Chris also shared some profitability statistics and explained that because of that, Ambit is ready to pour even more money into the field. When you read the numbers they will astound you. That leads to our kick off with Double/Triple Bonus. It is good through February 26th (Have to end on a Friday to keep the pay weeks straight). If that has not already got you working like never before, let me share some of the numbers with you.

Ambit ran the Exact Same Promotion in October 2009. Results:

- Highest number of new consultants ever.

- Highest number of new customers ever.

- Over $2,000,000 paid out to the consultants (Highest Ever).

- Triggering (Consultants joining Ambit and getting customers in 28 days to release bonus), reached an all time high.

- Texas – 77% of all new consultants triggered. 60% with Triple Bonus!!!!

- NY – 88% of new consultants with ALMOST ALL TRIGGERING DOUBLE BONUS (Call someone in NY!!!)

- IL – In between the numbers for Texas and NY, with the highest trigger ever

- Largest increase to Residual Income Customer Base ever in Ambit.

That brings us to **right now**:

The holidays are behind us. America is still reeling from the worst recession ever and Ambit is poised to become the Fastest Growing Company in America.

You own a business in the company that will make history in 2010. Ambit will be eligible for the Inc. 500 (Hint, Hint), and many other newspapers, magazines etc. will pick up on our incredible growth. They will be gracing us with FREE promotion for YOUR BUSINESS!

Other MLMs are suffering as Auto-ship and unnecessary products take a hit. As Americans seek to save money and WE SAVE THEM MONEY on services they can't live without!!!

Ambit is ready to pay us more than ever before. Way beyond the already most lucrative compensation plan around.

Our Top Leaders and Executives are on tour to spread the word and teach you how to take advantage of WHERE YOU ARE RIGHT NOW!

How to get the most out of the Double/Triple Bonus:

Don't focus on customer gathering! (Yes, I mean that.)

Teach new consultants to make a list and invite everyone to take a look at the Ambit Business opportunity. Learn to toggle from consultant to customer gathering on any prospect that hesitates or says no or not right now.

Did you get that?

Always ask people to be consultants and I assure you, many will not be ready. Simply ask them to be your customer and they will do so in part so you don't bug them about the business anymore. After they see the savings and travel incentives for themselves, they will be more ready to look at the business.

Big time success is just that simple. However, many of you reading this will say, "I can't do that. I need them to focus on customers first so both them and I get my bonus". The result, one bonus and a very slow growing team. We average 4 to 5 real customers per consultant. You want more customers, then get more consultants. PERIOD! If you are concentrating on customer gathering, you just don't get it, and you won't get the Big Income. Yes, everyone needs to get a few customers and trigger the bonus, but you do so by concentrating on inviting people to look at the business and **JUST REMEMBER THAT IF THEY SAY NO OR NOT RIGHT NOW, ASK THEM TO BE YOUR CUSTOMER!** Quit chasing people. Make them a customer and move on. There are many more waiting.

You are responsible for getting your own customers and ensuring those you sponsor get theirs. If after a week they are not getting customers talk to them about toggling from Consultant Prospect to Customer. **Don't ever stop recruiting to get customers!**

I talk to folks all the time that put their focus on making sure everyone triggers. Then they ask me why they can't earn the big money. I call that a clue! A customer is someone that says no or not right now to the business. Get your horse in front of your cart, and you will quickly fill your cart with customers. Our workhorse is the Consultant!

I wish each of you the best of success in your Ambit Business. I will be at each Launch Event to help you learn the Secrets to Success. But, you have to make a decision right now, that you take responsibility for doing and teaching it correctly. Do so and enjoy the greatest success of your life. Or, get advice from someone that doesn't earn a fortune each year, and follow his or her advice. If you want big time success, follow in the footsteps of successful people. That is what I did. Look where it got me!

Thanks for all you do. Grab for your dreams, NOW!

Not working hard in Ambit Energy this year could be the GREATEST FINANCIAL MISTAKE OF YOUR LIFE. It is your choice.

Beginning of Something Really Big!

Here we are in the final week of one of the best promotions ever. Not only did we open Philly, but also Ambit is paying Triple Bonus in Texas and Double Everywhere Else. It is a rare promotion, especially since it coincides with the opening of a new state. I am so glad that I said yes to Ambit and have stayed focused during the Formulation/Concentration Years. I am more excited than ever about it right now! This is the beginning of Aggressive Expansion. These next few months and years will create a tremendous number of Cash Millionaires from Ambit Energy. There has never been a better time.

Our first 4 1/2 years were tuff, exciting, stressful and Successful. They set the foundation for a much larger Level of Success. Our company is debt free, profitable and beyond sound. Just being named the #1 Fastest Growing Privately Held Company in America has lit the fuse and the rocket is burning even hotter. Many would say we have already been successful. I say we have been successful at getting off to a great start and building a Great Foundation! We are now ready to grow larger, faster and become an even better company while on our way to changing the history of MLM. We are making history and I am proud to be a part of that. I invite you to join us as we pick up speed and begin to set individuals Financially free at an even faster pace.

But first, you must get your house in order. **You must prepare yourself for success**, or it may elude you. Even with Ambit Energy, one of the Fastest Vehicles to Financial Freedom that ever existed, you could find yourself walking around the car, taking short test drives or even just gazing at it while parked. It is not difficult, but there are a few basic skills. The good news is that you can teach yourself the needed skills quickly!

First, you must give yourself permission to Succeed. We all have a history of being told it won't work or that it won't work for us, but it is just not true. Some of my closest Friends & Family said it would not work and in just a few short years many of us have become Financially Free. Like crabs in a barrel, your peers sometimes just try to pull you back down. That is why the say, "Misery Loves Company". Well say no! Not just to misery but to not reaching your full potential! Say yes to Success, not just with wishes and affirmations, but also with the consistent Declaration that you will be "Financially Free and Will Take Massive Action" toward that goal until it is **yours**! Declare that you will help so many others that your success is a given! Declare that over the next few years, you will change the future of your life and your family's lives for generations to come.

Next, you must commit. Now that you have committed to yourself, commit to Ambit, your prospects and fellow consultants. Commit that you will become a part of the system that sets so many free. Commit that you will make the calls, give the invitations and expose two or three people a day to The Ambit Opportunity until success is yours. The "Law of Large Numbers Will Work For You or Against You, But It Will Work." So, you need the numbers on your side. Not all at once, but a consistent two or three a day will bring about tremendous results.

Here is how it goes:

1) 7 or 8 of every 10 people you invite just won't look! Get over it. Don't spend too much time with the wrong people!

2) 1 or 2 out of every 4 that look will care enough to get all of the information and at least 1 of them will usually register as a consultant.

Help those people make a prospect list, make a few calls, get their first paycheck and get to training and you are on your way.

When some of them slow down or quit working --and they will -- spend your time with the ones that are working. **Work with those that deserve your help, not those that want your help!**

Never let management of your team get in the way of continuing to recruit. Lead from the front. Set the example. At the end of each workday ask: "If my whole Team did what I did today would it be a great day". If not, make your declaration to do it better tomorrow!

Focus on developing leaders and those leaders will earn you a fortune. No other industry is set up so wonderfully as to reward you for teaching your best skills to others and sharing in the abundance that will come from that. Always give first, and try to give more in value than you receive.

And yes, YOU CAN!

Do It Now! This will happen with or without any one of us. You make the choice. Some will find Success quickly. Others will take longer, but only the quitters fail.

Get Excited, Stay Focused and Never Ever Quit!

Making the Holidays Work For You

Greetings to all at this Wonderful Time to give thanks!

It has been a wonderful couple of years in Ambit Energy. It has been exciting for all of us as we are the Pioneers of not just Ambit Energy, but the Evolution of the Industry. We are nearly up to the ground floor now, so get ready to start working with all the New Folks that are about to "Get in on the Ground Floor!" (We are almost up to the Ground Floor).

That's right. More people will join Ambit in the next year than in the past two plus years. Dramatically More! Those Consultants will join the Team of the Leaders that Get Excited, Stay Focused and Never Ever Quit! Now is not the time to rest on our past, as the Big Game is Just beginning! New consultants will join this year and grow tremendous Teams, FAST!

We are the Industry Leader now, so there are others jumping in to our industry to try and grab a piece of the market. Most do not have the Financial or Management Strength to weather the storms and make a lasting impact. They look exciting, as it is always exciting to be first, but remember, Ambit Made It! We are the Industry Leader, about to open our 4th state. Sure others say they open half the universe at once, but that just reflects on the Management Skill. It is our methodical expansion that allows you and I to have an impact, territory by territory. The key is that it Allows, not Gives.

It takes total focus to become hugely successful. Now that you have chosen #1, stay focused and find your success. Every time you move, you have to start over and the only guarantee is that Ambit is strong enough to weather the toughest economic times in our lifetime. It is going to take that financial strength, with Jere and Chris's Leadership, to find sunshine in this storm. I am so glad I chose right and **NO ONE IS GOING TO STEAL MY FOCUS!** Congratulations. Just like me, you find yourself in a company where everyone else wants what we have!

And it is with Electricity & Natural Gas!

Well here we are in the Holiday Season. It is definitely a time to Give Thanks, but not the time to rest. Why do I say that? Isn't it true that in all of the MLM Industry the Holiday Season is the slowest? Yes it is true. Just like building a Space Shuttle is the slow time in Space Exploration. The Consultants that push and build harder now, position themselves for the greatest results in what comes in January, The Fastest Growth Time In The MLM Industry. Knowing this and taking action now, gives you a huge head start. It worked for me!

That's right. I started building my Ambit Business in November and December, the supposed "Slowest Time of the Year" That Massive Action durring the Holidays, positioned me for tremendous growth in the following year. My business achieved strong momentum while others were waiting out the "Slow Season". I credit that with a great deal of my success on the road to becoming a Top Money Earner. When others slow down, speed up! Then when others speed up, your larger group will be caught up in the momentum! **And massive success is all about momentum!**

As you have more success, more and more companies will contact you. IT is like becoming a Professional Athlete. Everyone wants to add a Professional to their Team, especially the weaker teams! Be careful not to be led off to where you can be the leader of a Losing Team. Professional Athletes sometimes do that because of the Millions they receive for the move. But they know their career is short lived and there is no pay when they stop. We have decades of growth ahead of us, and if we stay with a Proven Winner, we will get paid for years after we stop playing as frequently.

My goal now, is to help as many people taste the success that I have been blessed with. Because it is you that allowed me that success, but it did not come without work. I have worked harder for the last two years than ever before in my life. I had to give up a lot of other activities for that short period of time, but now the blessings are endless. Are you willing to do what it takes to achieve a higher level of Success than you ever had before, or are you slowing down to invite Mediocrity?

Thanks to the many new friends I have met and worked with over the last two years in Ambit. I look forward to meeting many new people and watching some of you become great leaders, living your dreams. Guess who gets to make that choice?

So, Happy Thanksgiving. I am thankful for all of you and for this great country and world we live in. I am very Thankful for the Ambit Success and will not take it lightly. There is plenty of room at the Top, so help lift your neighbor and yourself out of the crowded bottom land, and come Climb the Mountain with us.

Summer Slowdown

I have been hearing about Summer Slowdown for many years. Not just in MLM, but in my Insurance Career as well. It is amazing how widely that EXCUSE spreads! A few years ago I decided to buck that trend and see what it would change. The change was worth it!

When Ambit Launched New York on June 1 a couple of years ago, there was a flurry of activity for a couple of weeks. Then most of the "Traveling Ambit Leaders" apparently decided to stay home for the summer. I did not, but rather I increased my activity. I spent every other week that summer in NYC working with everyone I could. On the alternate week I was not off, but barnstorming around Texas doing the same thing. It seemed like tough times and everyone questioned and even made fun of how hard I was working. After all, it was "Summer Slowdown".

The result was that I went into Ambition as one of the Top Money Earners with more Team at Ambition than most. Sure enough, the announcements, training and excitement of Ambition set off and Explosion of Momentum and Activity all over Ambit. That is when leverage kicks in. Since our Team had worked harder in the "Summer Slowdown", we exploded in the fall. That November was the first time in my life to earn over $100,000 Dollars in a single month. Accident? Coincidence? I don't think so. Like a good friend of mine always says. "Success is a Choice." We made the right choice and that few months of hard work, against the tide of "Summer Slowdown", set me free.

No Decision is a Decision! We all love summer activities, but this is a business where you give up some things for a short period of time in order to have it all later. It sure is unlikely that you can skip that first part and just skip your way to Financial Freedom. Think twice when you are deciding about the Ambit Presentation or the ball game/picnic/lake/summer outing. What is the real, long-term cost of that choice? A few years ago I made the choice to skip a few summer outings with friends, and now I decide between my pool, ranch or just jetting off to somewhere wonderful. What has changed for you in the last few years? **How do you want your life to be a few years from now?**

Enjoy your summer, but not haphazardly. Make a firm plan and commitment to your future first. Commit to your Ambit Schedule and then fit in some summer fun. Pay yourself first so your future does not come in last. I am so glad I continued to struggle and work even while others played. It has changed my life forever.

Good luck in your Ambit Business. But take a lot of the luck out of the equation by making and keeping a plan for success! Don't hope it happens, MAKE IT HAPPEN! You have to try, fail, try again and succeed. It is the formula for Success.

PS: Many do not know that I was not one of the ten contacted and invited to Ambit by Chris and Jere. As a matter of fact, it was a few months later when I came in on the 3rd level. I made the choice to ask myself to be at the Top and be a Top Money Earner. I said yes to myself, and kept the commitment. You can too!

What an Exciting Time

What an exciting time in Ambit. Our production has already more than doubled since Ambition and it is just picking up speed. Make sure you are doing all that you can to get the most out of the Momentum and the Double/Triple and if you were at Ambition, the Level Up Bonus!

Next month I will celebrate the 6th Birthday of my Ambit Business. Although I have had other successes in my business life, there have been none like Ambit Energy. I was not always right when I chose new ventures, but I was always working and failing my way to knowledge, skill and success. You only have to be right one time, and we were right when we chose Ambit Energy! I know from my experience that an opportunity like this will probably never occur again. To find it is a blessing. To take massive action is to reach for all of your dreams in life. What we do for the next few years will (and for many of us, has) change our families lives for generations to come.

I share this now, after our 5th Ambition as we open the other coast. That is the first step in taking the country. I want so much for each of you to find the joy and Success that I have, in helping others reach for the sky. **DO NOT LET THIS PASS YOU BY.** Little efforts each day will compound dramatically. Massive Action over a several year period of time will change the course of your history. We all have it in our hands right now. We must act on it right now!

I am thankful each day for the blessings I continue to receive and for the thousands of people that made it possible and are now enjoying those blessings with me. Some of us are in the twilight of our career. It happens just that quickly, if you go for it. For most, the sun is just rising. Seize the opportunity. Make it yours. Do today what others won't, and you will have tomorrow what others don't.

I am strapping on my tool belt and expect to help make this the best year ever. I have dreamed of and worked toward this time in Business Life, forever. It is here. It is now. Come with me and this year we will change many thousands of lives.

Some will let this pass by. Many will watch it go by. Some will make it happen. You choose.

See you all over Ambit Land.

Get Excited.   **Stay Focused.**   **Never Quit!**

24

My Personal Wish For You

*T*hanks for sharing some time with me by reading this book. It is filled with real life information that has helped me reach for my dreams. It is my hope that in some way the information and stories from my life will help you to achieve your dreams.

Please do not make these ideas your exclusive advantage in the market place. Please share these ideas along with the best of everything you learn. If you share by giving away your best knowledge and ideas, or business practices or skills, it will come back to you many fold. All ships rise in a high tide and together, we can help millions to rise.

Many people and their generous sharing, have blessed me. I have been blessed with the ability to positively affect the lives of others and I am not only grateful but feel the responsibility to share and pay it forward. My hope is that you will join us in this goal and the wonderful journey that awaits you as you grow to have your own, "View From the Top".

Made in the USA
Lexington, KY
18 July 2013